EVERYBODY'S FAVORITE

Tastes may vary. Cooking styles may vary. Shopping budgets may vary. Dietary and nutritional concerns may vary. But on one thing every homemaker can agree. Whether you're serving an elegant dinner, a down-to-earth meal, or a simple hearty snack, chicken is the perfect answer to your needs.

Together with invaluable information ranging from how to cut up a chicken, or bone chicken parts, to the essential basic steps of various methods of preparation and a great variety of recipes, this is a guide that is both wonderfully up-to-date and of truly long-lasting value to any cooking library.

Everybody wins in the National Chicken Cooking Contest!

If you develop new chicken recipes for the competition, you have stimulated and furthered your creative cookery talents.

If your recipe gets you into a state or the national cook-off, you have an exciting experience and a chance to win big prizes.

If you use the recipes that are published through contest publicity, you have found some more interesting ways to enjoy chicken.

The contest starts with people sending us recipes for broiler-fryer chicken. Through judging and testing procedures and preliminary cook-offs, one person from each state and the District of Columbia is chosen to cook his or her own recipe in the national competition. Top prize at the national event is $10,000.

A winning recipe must be five things. It must be: 1) simple enough to appeal to most people, 2) different enough to excite one's interest, 3) contain varying ingredients that are familiar and readily available nationally, 4) look appealing, and 5) taste good. Each point is of equal value.

This book brings you all of the recipes being cooked in the 1975 national finals as well as general information about chicken and some basic preparation methods. There are also some favorite recipes from previous contest years.

We hope this book will bring you more pleasure from cooking and eating chicken and will inspire you to send us your special idea for cooking broiler-fryer chicken.

Anne

ANNE NESBITT, DIRECTOR
National Chicken Cooking Contest

THE CHICKEN COOKBOOK

POPULAR LIBRARY • NEW YORK

CONTENTS

BONUS: Your Entry Coupon for the 1976 National
       Chicken Cooking Contest precedes Index

A whole broiler-fryer is 53% edible meat. A 3-pound bird yields approximately 3 cups cooked edible meat. In an average 3-pound broiler-fryer:

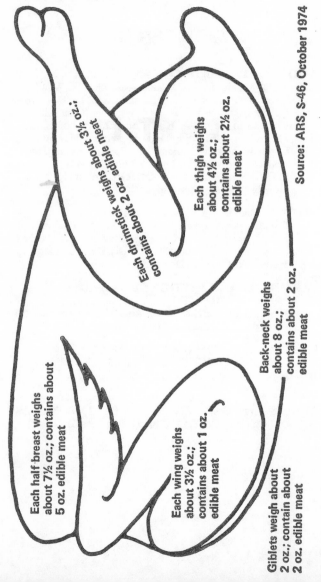

Source: ARS, S-46, October 1974

Each drumstick weighs about 3½ oz.; contains about 2 oz. edible meat

Each thigh weighs about 4½ oz.; contains about 2½ oz. edible meat

Each half breast weighs about 7½ oz.; contains about 5 oz. edible meat

Each wing weighs about 3½ oz.; contains about 1 oz. edible meat

Back-neck weighs about 8 oz.; contains about 2 oz. edible meat

Giblets weigh about 2 oz.; contain about 2 oz. edible meat

PART I

All About Chicken

TODAY'S CHICKEN—A MODERN MIRACLE

In most homes chicken appears at the family dinner table at least once—and oftentimes more—each week. And it's no wonder! In spite of rising food prices, chicken remains a "best buy." And its delicate flavor makes it a food popular with every member of the family.

To appreciate fully just what a good value today's chicken is, read on. Chicken is truly a modern miracle.

WHAT'S IN IT FOR YOU—NUTRITION

Lots of us are concerned about the nutritive value of what we eat. We want food which supplies protein, vitamins and minerals. Many of us are attempting to reduce our intake of fat, because of concern about overweight or for other health reasons. Few foods duplicate chicken's nutritive profile.

If you study the chart below you will learn what chicken contributes to your good health. Its nutrient values vary according to the part you select, but in every case the message is "full speed ahead."

NUTRITIVE CONTENT OF VARIOUS CHICKEN PARTS*

	Half Breast	Drumstick	Thigh	Wing	4 oz. Livers
Protein (grams)	27.6	12.8	15.4	5.1	22.3
Fat (grams)	3.2	2.6	4.8	2.1	4.2
Calories	147.7	78.2	108.7	40.6	146.2
Carbohydrate (grams)	—	—	—	—	3.3

* Source: *Food*, The Yearbook of Agriculture, 1959, USDA

9

PERCENTAGE OF RECOMMENDED DAILY ALLOWANCE FOR CHICKEN PARTS*

	Half Breast	Drumstick	Thigh	Wing	Liver
Vitamin A	2.0	1.7	3.1	1.3	274.5
Thiamine	4.5	3.0	3.3	.7	14.3
Riboflavin	12.4	12.7	16.6	2.3	166.2
Niacin	52.9	14.6	24.1	5.7	61.2
Iron	8.7	6.1	7.5	1.6	44.7
Calcium	1.5	.9	1.0	.3	.1
Phosphorus	28.7	12.6	15.8	5.6	26.7
Protein	61.9	27.9	34.2	11.5	49.5

Worth noting: The very high nutritive value of chicken livers; the bountiful supply of niacin in chicken breast meat; the excellent amounts of protein and the very low ratio of fat.

There's more to the chicken nutrition story.

Enthusiastic dieters often discard the skin of chicken before cooking, since they have heard that this will reduce the fat content. While it is true that most of the fat in chicken is concentrated just below the skin, even the skin of chicken is valuable nutritionally. Look at this comparison with steak and frankfurters:

FOR EDIBLE PORTION OF 100 GRAMS, RAW*

Nutrient	Chicken Skin	Sirloin	Frankfurter
Calories	223	313	296
Protein	16.1 gm.	16.9 gm.	13.1 gm.
Fat	17 gm.	26.7 gm.	25.5 gm.
Calcium	9 mg.	10 mg.	7 mg.
Phosphorus	174 mg.	155 mg.	133 mg.
Iron	2.4 mg.	2.5 mg.	1.9 mg.
Vitamin A	550 I.U.	50 I.U.	—
Thiamine	.03 mg.	.07 mg.	.16 mg.
Riboflavin	.13 mg.	.15 mg.	.20 mg.
Niacin	2.0 mg.	4.0 mg.	2.7 mg.

* Source: *Food,* The Yearbook of Agriculture, 1959, USDA

It's plain to see that chicken skin is low in fat compared to other commonly eaten meats. It's only necessary to remove the skin if an extremely low fat diet is desired.

The Kind of Fat

Some of us are concerned about the balance of saturated vs. unsaturated fats. Here again, chicken is the good news choice. Chicken is lower in saturated fat than beef or pork. The actual composition:

Saturated fatty acids		34%*
Palmitic	26%	
Stearic	7%	
Unsaturated fatty acids		66%
Oleic	40%	
Linoleic	21%	
Other	5%	

To make the comparison clear, the fat in cooked, regular ground hamburger is roughly 50% saturated.

It is interesting to note that linoleic acid is needed by the body for growth and reproduction.

What About Sodium?

Chicken is suitable for use in low sodium diets. A 100-gram edible portion of raw chicken without skin contains 50 milligrams of sodium in light meat, 67 milligrams for the dark meat.

Digestibility

Because chicken is a short-fibered meat it is easy to digest. This is important when feeding youngsters, older people, or those with digestive difficulties or upsets. People on bland ulcer diets, or who require soft foods, respond very well to chicken's tender texture, mild flavor and ready digestibility.

Low-Calorie Diets

Chicken is the calorie counter's ray of sunshine. Compared with other popular meats, chicken ranks lowest in

* Source: *Food,* The Yearbook of Agriculture, 1959, USDA

calories! A 3-ounce portion of skinless broiled chicken breast has only 115 calories; even with the skin left on, the calorie count is only 185. An equivalent size serving of roast pork has 310 calories, hamburger has 245 calories, and other meats have even higher counts.

Chicken takes well to low-calorie flavor additions in cooking. Herbs, fresh vegetables and fruits are good examples. The chicken dinner, thoughtfully prepared, is a dieter's paradise. Enjoy it!

The Big Picture

It should be clear that chicken offers a remarkable balance of nutrients. Most important, it is an excellent source of high-quality protein, rich in the essential amino acids that are indispensable for building, maintaining and replacing the body's tissues, muscles and cells. And this is teamed with the characteristic of being low in saturated fats, and lower than most meats in total fat content. Yet chicken contains enough fat so that other fats need not be added for palatability. This makes it ideal for all those watching total fat content. Just one more feature which makes chicken a modern miracle!

A LITTLE BACKGROUND—HOW CHICKEN GETS TO YOU

From beginning to end, getting chickens into your food market is an exercise in sanitation and careful judgment on the part of hundreds of inspectors.

Before the day's processing begins, every plant and every piece of equipment is inspected thoroughly. In addition, each and every chicken is scrutinized carefully, inside and out. Most inspections are conducted by the federal government; others are under state systems with similar standards.

Some of the chickens you buy will be marked with an inspection circle on the label or on package inserts, wing tags or giblet wrap. Sometimes chickens are delivered to the stores in large boxes. The boxes then carry the inspection mark, although individual birds may not.

Perhaps the chicken has been cut up and packaged at a

processing plant; if so, it will probably bear a brand name. Other chicken is cut up and packaged by the retailer. The cutting up is done systematically, using modern production line methods. Therefore when you buy a packaged cut-up chicken, all the pieces may not be from the same bird. As you know, chicken is sold by weight. So if a giblet or part is occasionally missing from a package the consumer is not charged for it.

Market Forms

There are four principle ways that chicken is delivered to the retail store.

Ice Pack birds are plucked, eviscerated and USDA inspected, chilled and shipped fresh, packed in containers filled with shaved ice. A similar process, called CO_2 pack, uses carbon dioxide "snow" as the refrigerant.

Deep Chill, Chill Pack or Crystal Pack the chicken is rapidly cooled to 28° to 32° but not frozen. Usually chickens processed by this method are packaged by the processor and shipped to the retailer without ice in refrigerated trucks. Some crystals may form when the birds are put in retail display cases. However, the birds do not "feel frozen"—you can depress the surface of the skin with your fingers.

Frozen Chicken is quick-frozen at the processing plant, shipped and sold frozen. Frozen chicken may be whole, in parts or even precooked.

Fresh, Fully Cooked as a convenience to their customers, delicatessen departments of supermarkets and fast-food concerns offer chicken fried, pan fried, roasted or barbecued. A true timesaver.

No matter what process is used to bring your chicken to market, you will be rewarded with a delicious meal. For best results, thaw frozen chicken in the refrigerator (see page 14). If the packaged chicken bears the label "ready to cook," this means you can start cooking as soon as the chicken is removed from the package.

What Kind of Chicken to Buy

Whole Birds are cleaned inside and out, are free of pinfeathers and eviscerated. The head, feet and inedible organs have been removed before weighing. The giblets (liver, gizzard and heart) have been washed, trimmed and wrapped; they are usually found inside the body cavity. When you are buying chicken with bone in, allow ¾ pound per person. A 3-pound bird serves four.

Broiler-fryers are the most popular size. They range in weight from 2 to 3½ pounds.

Roasting Chickens weigh more and are meaty and tender, with enough fat to brown well at roasting temperatures.

Hens, Stewing Chickens and Fowls are mature, less tender chickens, ranging in weight from 2½ to 8 pounds. They are best cooked by simmering for dishes like soup, chicken fricassee or stew, or for meat to be used in creamed dishes and salads.

Capons are tender and have lots of white meat. They are usually roasted, and weigh from 5 to 8 pounds.

Rock Cornish Hens are 1 to 2 pounds in weight. Usually sold frozen, they may be roasted, or cooked on the rotisserie. Halved hens can be broiled, fried or baked. A 1-pound bird serves one, a 1½- to 2-pound bird serves two.

Broiler-fryer Chickens, Cut in Parts, save you time when you are planning to serve the chicken in pieces. You may want to use wing tips, backs and giblets to make simmered chicken or broth, and use the meatier portions for frying, baking or top-of-stove simmering.

Chicken Halves cook faster than the whole bird. Allow one chicken half per person. They may be baked, broiled, simmered or barbecued.

Chicken Quarters may also be purchased. Allow one quarter per person—two for Dad, perhaps!

Drumsticks make good finger food. They weigh about 3½ ounces each. Two make one serving.

Thighs are meaty portions of dark meat. You may bone them for fancy dishes. About 4 ounces each, two to a serving.

Chicken Breasts are available whole or split. Breasts range between 12 and 15 ounces each. One half breast is a serving.

14

Wings are often trimmed and the meatier portions served as party hors d'oeuvres. These are called drummettes, wingettes, or something similar. Each wingette weighs almost 2 ounces. Count on 3 per serving.

Boneless Skinless Breasts are becoming popular. This elegant cut is often substituted for more expensive veal cutlet. They may be called chicken cutlets.

Chicken Giblets include gizzard, liver and heart. Since these are boneless, allow ¼ pound per serving. Chicken livers are often sold separately and may be used in a variety of tempting, nutritious dishes.

How Long Does Chicken Stay Fresh?

It's usually just a matter of hours after the chicken has been inspected that it appears in the retail store's food case. When kept under refrigeration the chicken will retain maximum quality in the store for seven days or more.

In some localities chickens are "open-dated": the package will bear a legend "sell by (date)."

Fresh tray-packed chicken should not be kept more than two days in the coldest part of the home refrigerator to maintain maximum quality. If you plan to keep it for a longer period you should freeze it.

Multiple-bagged chickens or parts should be rinsed, patted dry with paper towels, separated into portions desired and repacked in clean bags or other packaging materials.

Freezing Chicken

Uncooked chicken may be frozen whole or in parts. Use moisture-vapor-resistant material suitable for freezing. This includes heavy-duty foil, freezer paper and plastic freezer bags of good quality. Be sure to press the air out of each package and seal well. Home frozen fresh chicken kept at 0° will retain its palatability for 4 to 6 months. Commercially frozen chicken, wrapped and stored under the most favorable conditions, may be kept 12 months.

Cooked chicken, whole or in parts, is frozen using the same techniques and materials as fresh raw chicken. If the cooked chicken is in a gravy or sauce, use a rigid container with a tight-fitting lid.

Cooked chicken may be kept in the home freezer for 2 months.

Thawing Chicken

Thaw chicken in the refrigerator with the wrapping loosened. Whole frozen chickens under 4 pounds require 12 to 16 hours to thaw. Chicken pieces need 4 to 9 hours in the refrigerator. Chicken may be thawed more rapidly by placing chicken, bag and all, in cold water.

It is not considered wise to refreeze either cooked or uncooked chicken once it has been thawed. Each successive thawing and refreezing lowers quality.

A Timesaving Trick

If you plan to bake chicken parts, or perhaps to poach them in liquid, you will not need to thaw them providing you packaged them properly for the freezer.

Place each chicken part in its own plastic bag, press out air and seal well. Freeze separately. The parts can then be gathered together and placed in a large plastic or stockinet bag for long-term storage.

When parts are needed, take out just the number you need, remove from wrapping and place in hot liquid or in a baking pan in the oven. If the chicken is to be baked or simmered, you'll find the parts are cooked in about the same time whether they are frozen or thawed when you begin. However, if you are baking a frozen chicken casserole dish you should allow from 15 to 30 minutes' extra baking time (compared to the same recipe not frozen).

Cooked Chicken Pointers

Planning a picnic or box lunch? Then you will want to know how long chicken will keep without refrigeration.

If the chicken is cooked with *no sauce*—that is, just fried, baked or broiled—it may be cooled rapidly in the refrigerator. It is then safe at room temperature for up to 4 hours at 70° to 75°. If the day is warmer, it's best to wrap the cold chicken in foil or plastic, then in several layers of newspapers, to keep it cold. Or use an insulated container or ice chest.

Chicken salad or creamed chicken or any recipe containing a sauce should *always* be refrigerated until eating time.

Never stuff a chicken and put it in the refrigerator until the next day, or even for several hours. If you want to work ahead, make the stuffing and put it in a flat pan in the refrigerator. When you're ready to roast, stuff the chicken and pop it into the oven at once.

After you have served the chicken, remove any leftover stuffing to a covered container and refrigerate. Cover and refrigerate gravy separately. Wrap the bird in transparent plastic film and refrigerate. Use everything within 2 to 3 days.

When Is Chicken Done?

In the recipes that follow you will find time guides. These should be followed for best results. In general, chicken is cooked when its juices are no longer pink but run clear.

Occasionally, after the chicken is thoroughly cooked, you may spot an unusual color.

Sometimes the meat near the bones darkens. This is caused by a reaction within the bone structure which occurs during slow freezing. (Freezing chicken at home is slow compared to what is done commercially.) This darker meat is just as good tasting and healthful as the rest of the bird.

Occasionally, even though the chicken is fully cooked, the meat next to the bone is pink. This is due to the reaction of natural nitrogen-containing material during the cooking. In spite of the pink color the chicken is quite well done.

Good Tests for Doneness

Chicken is done when fork tender (fork inserted with ease).

17

Chicken is done when thick muscle of drumstick feels soft to finger touch.

Chicken is done when the leg moves readily when lifted or twisted.

Chicken is done when meat thermometer inserted into thickest part of thigh muscle registers 190°F.

Chicken is done when the thermometer inserted in the stuffing registers 165°F.

A Rule to Follow

Many of us cut up chicken ourselves (see page 19), since this can save considerable money. And frequently we cut or pound chicken before cooking it.

Home economists tell us that whenever you handle raw chicken (or indeed any uncooked protein food), the surfaces which it has contacted should be cleaned before you go on to any other food preparation. This means scrubbing knives and other utensils with detergent, and rinsing well, as well as washing your hands thoroughly. Scrub the cutting board with a cleanser containing chlorine bleach, and rinse and dry well. You might investigate the new cutting boards made of plastic or ceramic; these are easy to keep clean.

Never put cooked food back on a platter or tray on which raw meat has been placed prior to cooking without washing the platter or tray.

HOW TO CUT UP
A WHOLE CHICKEN

Buying a whole broiler-fryer will save you money every time.
To cut up the bird the professional way, follow these easy
step-by-step directions.

1. Begin by cutting off
   legs. Cut skin be-
   tween thighs and
   body of chicken.

3. Remove leg from
   body by cutting
   from back to front
   as close as possible
   to the back bone.

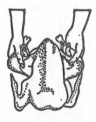

2. Lift chicken and
   bend legs, grasping
   one leg with each
   hand. Bend legs un-
   til hip joints are
   loose.

4. Then separate thigh
   and drumstick. Lo-
   cate joint by squeez-
   ing between thigh
   and drumstick. Cut
   through joint.

above the spoon-shaped bones in the back. Another method is to separate the back from the breast by cutting between the breast and back ribs from the shoulder to the tail end. Bend the back away from breast to separate the shoulder joints.

5. To remove wing from body, start cutting on inside of wing just over the joint. Cut down and around the joint. To make the wing lie flat, make a small cut on the inside of the large wing joint. Cut just deep enough to expose the bones. Repeat with wing on other side.

7. Place breast skin side down on cutting board. Cut through white cartilage at the V of the neck.

6. To cut the body into breast and back sections, place the chicken on neck end and cut from the tail along each side of back bone through rib joints to neck. Cut through the skin that attaches the neck-and-back strip to the breast. Place neck-and-back strip skin side up on cutting board. Cut into two pieces just

8. Hold breast firmly with both hands and bend back both sides. Push up with fingers to snap out the breastbone. Cut breast in half lengthwise.

20

HOW TO
REMOVE BONES FROM
A CHICKEN BREAST HALF

1. This is a whole breast, halved (cut in half).

2. Break joint at end of large bone which is about center of breast half.

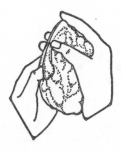

3. Run thumb under large bone.

4. Pull large bone away from meat.

7. Feel meat to be sure no small bones embedded.

5. Run thumb under small bones.

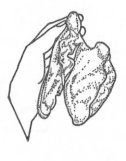

8. Pull skin off, if desired.

6. Pull small bones away from meat.

HOW TO BONE CHICKEN THIGHS

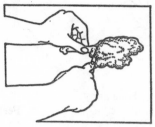

1. With skin side down and thin side up, slice top from joint to joint.

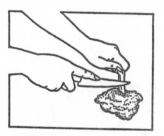

2. Cut near one joint to expose bone. Pull or scrape meat away.

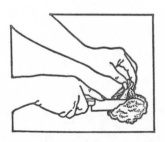

3. Cut meat from other joint. Pull off skin, if desired.

...cate flavorings make this familiar chicken dish very interesting. Perfect accompaniments: buttered asparagus and new...

It's also a good change you'll have all the ingredients on hand and for the most any favorite recipe that needs no previous cooking.

PART II
Back To Basics

COOKING KNOW-HOW

Although it's great fun to add your favorite flavors and produce unusual chicken dishes, there are times when you're hungry for just plain chicken—fried, roasted or even simmered. Then you will want to turn to this section of the book, which provides you with tried and true recipes for the simplest chicken dishes. The basic methods and time guides are also useful when you're inventing your own prize-winning recipes.

Fried Chicken

1 broiler-fryer chicken, cut in parts	1 teaspoon Ac'cent flavor enhancer
½ cup flour	⅛ teaspoon pepper
1 teaspoon salt	¼ cup Mazola corn oil
1 teaspoon paprika	

Mix flour, salt, paprika, flavor enhancer and pepper in a plastic or paper bag. Add chicken pieces, a few at a time, and shake until well coated. If there is time, let coating set by allowing chicken to dry on wire rack for 15 minutes. Heat corn oil in fry pan over medium heat. Add chicken, skin side down. Cook, uncovered, 15 to 25 minutes on each side, turning only once. Chicken is done when fork can be inserted with ease. Drain on paper towels. Makes 4 servings.

For a change: When preparing flour mixture, add ½ teaspoon dried leaf thyme, tarragon, basil or poultry seasoning, or 1 teaspoon curry powder.

Oven-Fried Chicken

Using proportions for fried chicken, coat broiler-fryer chicken parts with seasoned flour. Pour ¼ cup Mazola corn oil in foil-lined large shallow baking pan. Place coated chicken pieces, skin side down, in single layer in pan. Bake, uncovered, in 375° oven 25 minutes; turn and bake 20 minutes longer, until fork can be inserted with ease.

Oven-Fried Chicken, Another Way

Roll chicken pieces in ¼ cup Mazola corn oil, then roll in a mixture of ⅓ cup cracker meal, 1 teaspoon Ac'cent flavor enhancer, 1 teaspoon salt and ¼ teaspoon pepper. Bake in 375° oven 40 minutes, or until fork can be inserted with ease.

Broiled Chicken

Cut broiler-fryer into halves, quarters or pieces. Sprinkle with 1 teaspoon salt, ¼ teaspoon pepper and 1 teaspoon Ac'cent flavor enhancer. Brush with 2 table-spoons Mazola corn oil. Place skin side down on broiler rack. Set temperature control at broil or 450°. Arrange rack so chicken is 3 to 6 inches from heat in gas range or 6 to 9 inches from heat in an electric range. Broil 20 to 25 minutes. Repeat brushing with corn oil. Turn. Broil 15 to 20 minutes longer, or until fork can be inserted with ease.

Variation: Sprinkle the pieces with 2 tablespoons lemon juice and/or ½ teaspoon of an herb such as tarragon, thyme or basil.

Barbecued Chicken

Chicken may be cooked on an outdoor grill, using approximately the same methods as for broiled chicken. Commercially prepared or homemade barbecue sauce may be brushed on the chicken during the last 15 to 20 minutes of grilling time.

Roast Chicken

Choose a whole broiler-fryer. Sprinkle body cavity and outside of bird with 1 teaspoon salt and 1 teaspoon Ac'cent flavor enhancer. If desired, stuff body cavity with Basic Herb Stuffing or your favorite recipe, using 1¾ cups stuffing for broiler-fryer weighing 3½ pounds. Hook wing tips onto back to hold neck in place. Brush chicken with ¼ cup Mazola corn oil. Place chicken directly in shallow pan; it is not necessary to use a rack. Roast in 375° oven for approximately 1 hour, or until leg moves freely when lifted or turned. If bird is stuffed, add 15 minutes to total cooking time. An average broiler-fryer makes 4 servings.

Basic Herb Stuffing

⅓ cup Mazola corn oil	½ teaspoon salt
½ medium onion, chopped	½ teaspoon Ac'cent flavor
4 cups bread cubes	enhancer
½ cup chopped celery	¼ teaspoon pepper
¼ cup chopped parsley	

Heat corn oil in fry pan over medium heat. Add onion; saute until golden brown. Add remaining ingredients; toss. Makes about 3½ cups, enough for 2 broiler-fryers.

Simmered Chicken
(for salads, casseroles, creamed dishes)

1 broiler-fryer chicken, whole or cut in parts	1 teaspoon Ac'cent flavor enhancer
2 cups water	1 teaspoon salt
1 small onion, sliced	¼ teaspoon pepper
3 celery tops	

Place chicken in a deep saucepan. Add water and remaining ingredients. Bring to a boil. Cover tightly, reduce heat and simmer approximately 1 hour, or until fork can be inserted with ease. Remove from heat. Strain broth. Refrigerate chicken and broth at once. Chill. When chicken is cool, remove meat from skin and bones. Cut into chunks. A 3-pound broiler-fryer chicken will yield about 3 cups diced cooked chicken and 2 to 2½ cups broth.

Herb-Fried Chicken Drumsticks

36 broiler-fryer chicken
   drumsticks (about 9
   pounds)
4 teaspoons salt, divided
2 teaspoons Ac'cent flavor
   enhancer

3 cups flour
2 teaspoons paprika
2 teaspoons dried leaf
   thyme
1½ cups buttermilk
1 cup Mazola corn oil

Sprinkle drumsticks with 2 teaspoons salt and flavor enhancer. Mix together flour, remaining salt, paprika and thyme. Dip chicken in buttermilk; then roll in seasoned flour. Heat corn oil in fry pan over medium heat. Add drumsticks and cook, uncovered, 15 to 20 minutes on each side, turning only once. Drain well on absorbent paper. Makes 12 to 18 servings.

Note: Milk may be substituted for buttermilk (decrease flour to 2 cups), but buttermilk is thicker and holds more flour to make a firmer coating.

PART III
Great Recipes of
Previous Winners

A different kind of cracker with a seasoning of celery salt makes this fried chicken dish unforgettable.

DELMARVALICIOUS FRIED CHICKEN

1 broiler-fryer chicken, cut in parts
2 eggs, lightly beaten
2½ teaspoons salt
1 teaspoon Ac'cent flavor enhancer
2½ teaspoons celery salt
1 teaspoon paprika
½ teaspoon pepper
2 cups crushed buttery round crackers
1 cup Mazola corn oil

Mix together eggs, salt, flavor enhancer, celery salt, paprika and pepper. Dip chicken in this mixture, then roll in crushed crackers. Heat corn oil in deep fry pan over medium heat. Add chicken. Cook, turning frequently, uncovered, about 45 minutes, or until fork can be inserted with ease. Makes 4 servings.

1950—Eleanor Clark, Easton, Maryland

Pumpkin pie spice adds an unusual fragrance to this easy fry pan recipe. Mint imparts a fresh taste.

HONEYMINT SPICED CHICKEN

1 broiler-fryer chicken, cut in serving pieces
½ cup flour
2 teaspoons salt
1 teaspoon Ac'cent flavor enhancer

¼ cup Mazola corn oil
⅓ cup honey
1 teaspoon dehydrated mint leaves
½ teaspoon pumpkin pie spice

Mix flour, salt and flavor enhancer in bag. Add chicken, one piece at a time, and shake to coat. Heat corn oil in fry pan over medium heat. Add chicken and brown on all sides. Mix together honey, mint and pumpkin pie spice. With chicken skin side down, brush one-half of honey mixture on pieces. Cover and cook over medium heat for 15 minutes. Turn chicken; brush on remainder of mixture. Cover and continue cooking another 15 minutes or until done. Garnish with mandarin orange slices sprinkled with a dash of pumpkin pie spice and fresh mint sprigs. Makes 4 servings.

1968—Mrs. Robert J. Reiners, Glenshaw, Pennsylvania

Corn flakes make an interesting, crisp coating for fried chicken.

FRIED CHICKEN-DELMARVA 1952

1 broiler-fryer chicken, cut in parts	1 teaspoon Ac'cent flavor enhancer
1 egg, slightly beaten	1½ cups crushed corn flakes
1 tablespoon water	1 cup Mazola corn oil
2 teaspoons salt	½ teaspoon pepper

In a shallow bowl, mix together egg, water, salt and flavor enhancer. Dip chicken in this mixture; roll in corn flake crumbs, coating well. Heat corn oil in chicken fryer or dutch oven over medium heat. Add chicken and cook slowly, uncovered, turning occasionally to brown and cook evenly, about 45 minutes or until fork can be inserted with ease. During the cooking, sprinkle pieces with pepper. Makes 4 servings.

1952—Mrs. Floyd Kerns, Salisbury, Maryland

Do you love a spectacular? This recipe allows culinary dramatics before the eyes of your guests!

CHICKEN FLAMBÉ

2 broiler-fryer chickens, quartered
2 teaspoons Ac'cent flavor enhancer
2 teaspoons salt
¼ teaspoon pepper
¼ cup Mazola corn oil
⅔ cup dry white wine
2 tablespoons flour
1 cup water
6 tablespoons brandy

Sprinkle flavor enhancer, salt and pepper on chicken. Heat corn oil over medium heat in fry pan from which chicken can be served. Add chicken and brown on both sides. Add wine; cover and simmer 45 minutes, or until fork can be inserted with ease. Remove chicken pieces. Stir flour into drippings in pan, add water and bring to boil. Return chicken to pan. Add brandy, ignite, and serve blazing. Spoon sauce over chicken when serving. Makes 8 servings.

1957—Mrs. Ethel Davis, Wilmington, Delaware

All the flavors of an old-fashioned cocktail are captured in the marinade for these chicken pieces. The taste is sealed in while the chicken is gently fried. Something special!

DELMARVA-LICIOUS GOLDEN FRIED CHICKEN

2 broiler-fryer chickens, cut in parts	1 tablespoon lemon juice
1 tablespoon salt	1 tablespoon bourbon whiskey
2 teaspoons Ac'cent flavor enhancer	¼ cup water
1 teaspoon garlic salt	2 eggs, beaten
2 teaspoons paprika	½ cup flour
1 tablespoon aromatic bitters	1½ cups fine breadcrumbs
	1 cup Mazola corn oil

Mix together salt, flavor enhancer, garlic salt and paprika, and sprinkle on chicken. Place chicken in large shallow baking dish. Make sauce by mixing together bitters, lemon juice, bourbon whiskey and water in saucepan and heat to boiling. Pour sauce over chicken and marinate for 1 hour, turning frequently. Drain liquid from chicken and add liquid to beaten egg. Dip chicken in flour, then egg mixture, then crumbs. Heat corn oil in fry pan over medium heat. Add chicken and brown on all sides. Continue cooking, uncovered, approximately 45 minutes or until fork can be inserted with ease. Garnish with spiced apples or brandied peaches. Makes 8 servings.

1960—Mrs. Elizabeth Goetz, Lakewood, New Jersey

This stir-fry dish is prepared as thoughtfully as the best of the Chinese cuisine. It's just as attractive as it is mouth watering.

SPRINGTIME CHICKEN

3 whole broiler-fryer chicken breasts, boned, skinned and cut in 1-inch pieces

¼ cup Mazola corn oil, divided

2 slices ginger root (equivalent—¼ teaspoon ground ginger)

1 pound asparagus, fresh or frozen, cut in 1½-inch pieces (separate the tips)

2 green onions with tops, sliced

5 ounces fresh mushrooms, sliced

1½ teaspoons Ac'cent flavor enhancer

½ teaspoon salt

Heat 2 tablespoons of the corn oil with ginger in fry pan over medium heat. Add chicken, stirring constantly, frying 3 to 5 minutes or until chicken is done and becomes white and opaque. Add more oil if needed. Remove chicken from pan and keep warm by wrapping in foil. Discard ginger root if fresh ginger was used. Add remaining 2 tablespoons of corn oil to pan. When heated, add asparagus, excluding tips; stir fry about 2 minutes. Add asparagus tips, onions and mushrooms, stirring constantly for 1 to 2 minutes. (Asparagus should be bright green.) Return chicken to pan. Add Ac'cent flavor enhancer and mix. Heat, covered, about 1 minute, or until asparagus is tender crisp. Season to taste. Makes 4 to 6 servings.

1973—Miss Susan A. Bronczyk, Omaha, Nebraska

You will be surprised to discover how nicely the flavor of dried beef complements chicken. Men like this!

CHICKEN BREASTS SUPREME

2 whole broiler-fryer chicken breasts, halved, boned, skinned
⅓ cup flour
1 teaspoon Ac'cent flavor enhancer
½ teaspoon salt
¼ teaspoon ground black pepper

2 eggs
¾ cup fresh breadcrumbs
3 tablespoons grated Parmesan cheese
½ cup finely chopped dried beef
⅓ cup Mazola corn oil

Mix together flour, flavor enhancer, salt and pepper. In a pie plate or shallow dish, beat egg slightly. Mix together breadcrumbs, cheese and dried beef. Dip chicken breast in flour mixture, then dip in egg and coat with crumb mixture. Heat corn oil in fry pan over medium heat. Add chicken pieces. Cook over medium heat 10 minutes, turning once to brown on both sides. Reduce heat and cook 10 minutes, or until fork can be inserted with ease. Makes 4 servings.

Note: Dried beef may be done in the blender or in meat grinder, or chopped fine by hand.

1974—Mrs. Ben Bodell (Sara), Covington, Virginia

The Near Eastern flavor of this dish will tempt your guests. If everything is ready in advance you'll find it takes little time to cook.

HONG KONG CHICKEN

3 whole broiler-fryer chicken breasts, boned, skinned and cut in 1-inch pieces
¼ cup soy sauce
1 tablespoon sugar
1 tablespoon dry sherry
1½ teaspoons Ac'cent flavor enhancer
1 teaspoon salt
1 teaspoon corn starch
¼ teaspoon garlic powder

¼ teaspoon ground ginger
⅛ teaspoon pepper
⅓ cup Mazola corn oil, divided
2 green peppers, cut in ½-inch cubes (about 2 cups)
1 can (8½ ounces) sliced bamboo shoots, drained
2 tablespoons honey
½ cup cashew nuts

In a large bowl, mix together soy sauce, sugar, dry sherry, flavor enhancer, salt, corn starch, garlic powder, ginger and pepper. Add chicken and toss gently to coat pieces well. Drain chicken pieces and reserve liquid. Heat 2 tablespoons of the corn oil in a fry pan over medium heat. Add the chicken pieces; cook, uncovered, stirring constantly, until chicken is browned on all sides, about 5 to 7 minutes. Remove chicken from fry pan with a slotted spoon and place on platter. Cover with foil. Drain off any liquid in fry pan. Add the remaining corn oil to fry pan; heat. Stir in peppers, bamboo shoots and 2 tablespoons of the reserved soy sauce mixture. Cook, uncovered, until the peppers are tender crisp, about 3 to 4 minutes. Return the browned chicken to the fry pan and stir gently to combine with vegetable mixture. Add the honey and cook, uncovered, 2 to 3 minutes longer. Just before serving, add the cashews. Serve with rice. Makes 6 servings.

1973—Mrs. Lawrence Rudzinski (Linda), Centerville, Ohio

This inspired combination, colorful and flavorful, would be a good choice for a dinner party for four.

CHICKEN AND SHRIMP ELEGANT

1 broiler-fryer chicken, cut in parts
7 tablespoons flour, divided
1½ teaspoons seasoned salt
½ teaspoon paprika
¼ teaspoon ground black pepper
¼ cup Mazola corn oil
1 cup chicken bouillon
1¼ cups dry white wine
1 teaspoon Ac'cent flavor enhancer

1 tablespoon dried chives
½ cup water
1½ cups (about 8 ounces) shelled, deveined shrimp
1 can (6 ounces) button mushrooms, drained
½ cup sliced olives with pimento
2 tablespoons minced parsley

Mix together 4 tablespoons of the flour, seasoned salt, paprika and pepper. Coat chicken pieces. Heat corn oil in fry pan over medium heat. Add chicken and cook until evenly browned, turning once. Remove chicken, set aside. Drain excess fat. Pour bouillon and wine into fry pan. Cook over low heat 5 minutes, scraping pan. Add flavor enhancer and chives. Mix 3 tablespoons flour with water until smooth. Slowly stir mixture into fry pan, stirring constantly, and cook 5 minutes, or until sauce is smooth and thickened. Return chicken to fry pan. Cover; cook 30 minutes over low heat, turning chicken occasionally. Gently stir shrimp, mushrooms, olives and parsley into pan. Cover; cook over low heat 10 minutes, or until fork can be inserted with ease. Makes 4 servings.

1974—Mrs. James Gordon (Zelda), San Francisco, California

Sesame seeds bring out the nutty flavor of chicken. This dish will please guests and also goes over very well with children.

SESAME CHICKEN

4 whole broiler-fryer
  chicken breasts, halved,
  boned
1 egg, slightly beaten
½ cup flour, divided
1 teaspoon sugar
1 teaspoon Ac'cent flavor
  enhancer

1 teaspoon almond extract
½ teaspoon salt
¼ teaspoon baking powder
¼ teaspoon ground pepper
1 cup sesame seed
1 quart Mazola corn oil

Mix together egg, 1 tablespoon flour, sugar, flavor enhancer, almond extract, salt, baking powder and pepper to make a batter. Dip chicken pieces in batter; place on waxed paper. Sprinkle both sides with sesame seed. Coat with remaining flour. Heat corn oil in deep fryer or fry pan, over medium heat, until it reaches 375°. Carefully place the coated chicken pieces, a few at a time, into the hot corn oil. Cook 5 minutes, or until golden brown and chicken is done; drain on paper towels. Garnish with parsley. Makes 8 servings.

Note: Chicken pieces may be prepared and coated, then refrigerated overnight until just before serving time.

1974—Mrs. Simon Ho Chen (Rosemary), Delavan, Wisconsin

Grandma's chicken stew was never this elegant. Unless, of course, she came from France and brought its traditions with her!

WINE-GLAZED CHICKEN AND VEGETABLES

1 broiler-fryer chicken, quartered	⅛ teaspoon rosemary, crumbled
1 teaspoon Ac'cent flavor enhancer	2 tablespoons lemon juice
½ teaspoon salt	1 can (6 ounces) mushrooms, with liquid
¼ teaspoon ground pepper	½ cup chicken broth
¼ cup Mazola corn oil	½ cup red Burgundy wine
2 tablespoons flour	12 small onions, peeled
1 teaspoon sugar	1 pound baby carrots
⅛ teaspoon thyme leaves, crumbled	Parsley

Sprinkle chicken with flavor enhancer, salt and pepper. Heat corn oil in fry pan or dutch oven over medium heat. Add chicken, brown lightly, turning as needed. Remove chicken. Mix together flour, sugar, thyme and rosemary. Stir into pan drippings to make a smooth paste. Add lemon juice, mushroom liquid, broth; cook, stirring, until it boils. Add wine, onions, carrots, mushrooms and chicken. Reduce heat; cover and simmer 30 minutes. Remove cover and continue cooking at a higher heat until most liquid is evaporated and chicken and vegetables are coated with a thick, rich glaze. Garnish with parsley. Makes 4 servings.

1974—Mrs. Claude Swank (Lenore), Cassopolis, Michigan

What is especially nice about this recipe is the exciting spicing. Red wine gives the dish a little lift.

DRUNKEN MEXICAN CHICKEN
(Pollo Borracho)

1 broiler-fryer chicken, cut in parts	½ teaspoon cumin seed
1 teaspoon Ac'cent flavor enhancer	¼ teaspoon garlic powder
¼ cup Mazola corn oil	1 cube chicken bouillon, crushed
1¼ teaspoons salt	1 can (16 ounces) tomatoes, chopped
1 teaspoon paprika	1 large onion, sliced
¾ teaspoon ground black pepper	5 medium zucchini squash, sliced
½ teaspoon crushed oregano	1 cup red Burgundy wine

Sprinkle chicken with flavor enhancer. Heat corn oil in dutch oven over medium heat. Add chicken and brown well on all sides. Sprinkle in salt, paprika, black pepper, oregano, cumin, garlic powder and bouillon. Reduce heat to medium low; add tomatoes, onion, zucchini and wine. Cook, covered, 30 minutes; uncover and continue cooking another 15 minutes, or until liquid is somewhat reduced and the chicken is done. Makes 4 servings. Excellent served with brown rice, pinto beans and avocado fruit salad.

1974—Mrs. Arnold Israelit (Virginia), Dallas, Texas

Here's a recipe sure to please men. The combination of onion and hickory-smoked salt gives this indoor recipe an outdoor flavor. The superb barbecue sauce adds both brownness and an unforgettable taste.

SWEET 'N' SMOKY OVEN-BARBECUED CHICKEN

1 broiler-fryer chicken, quartered	¼ teaspoon pepper
1 large onion, sliced	1 teaspoon Ac'cent flavor enhancer
1 teaspoon hickory-smoked salt	

BARBECUE SAUCE

½ cup catchup	¼ cup vinegar
½ cup Mazola corn oil	2 tablespoons prepared mustard
½ cup maple syrup	

Place chicken, skin side up, in shallow baking pan. Tuck onion slices in and around the chicken. Sprinkle hickory-smoked salt, pepper and flavor enhancer on chicken. Bake, uncovered, in 375° oven for 30 minutes. Make barbecue sauce by mixing together ingredients listed. Pour barbecue sauce over chicken, and bake 30 minutes longer, or until fork can be inserted with ease. Makes 4 servings.

1966—Mrs. Laurence R. Martin, Wheeling, West Virginia

Had you ever thought of using Russian dressing as a cooking ingredient? It makes a very zesty glaze.

SWEET AND SOUR CHICKEN

2 broiler-fryer chickens, cut in parts
¼ cup Mazola corn oil
1 bottle (8 ounces) Russian salad dressing
1 envelope (1⅜ ounces) dry onion soup mix

1 jar (10 ounces) apricot preserves
1 teaspoon Ac'cent flavor enhancer
1 teaspoon salt

Mix together all ingredients except chicken. Place chicken in single layer, skin side up, in large shallow baking pan; pour preserves mix on chicken. Bake in 350° oven for 1 hour, or until fork can be inserted with ease, basting occasionally with the pan drippings. Serve hot with plain rice and the sweet and sour sauce. Makes 8 servings.

1969—Mrs. Cecil L. Smith, Westwood, Massachusetts

Just a touch of garlic gets this recipe off on the right foot. The combination of cheddar and Parmesan cheeses is exciting and appealing.

CHEESE DELIGHT IN EVERY BITE CHICKEN

3 whole broiler-fryer chicken breasts, halved and boned
1 clove garlic
½ cup Mazola corn oil
1 cup fine dry breadcrumbs
½ cup finely grated sharp cheddar cheese
¼ cup grated Parmesan cheese
1 teaspoon Ac'cent flavor enhancer
1 teaspoon salt
⅛ teaspoon pepper

Add garlic to corn oil and let stand 20 minutes. Remove garlic. Mix together breadcrumbs, cheeses, flavor enhancer, salt and pepper. Dip breast pieces in corn oil, then crumb mixture. Place in large shallow baking pan, tucking sides under to form neat roll. Be sure breast pieces do not touch each other. Pour remainder of corn oil over chicken pieces. Bake, uncovered, 350° oven approximately 45 minutes, or until fork can be inserted with ease. Baste occasionally with pan juices if desired. Makes 6 servings.

1970—Miss Kim Leslie Bowen, Vienna, Virginia

Amazingly simple, this recipe which bakes while you prepare the rest of your dinner. Good eating, too.

HONEY CHICKEN

1 broiler-fryer chicken, cut in parts	¼ teaspoon pepper
1 teaspoon Ac'cent flavor enhancer	¼ cup Mazola corn oil
	½ cup honey
1 teaspoon salt	2 tablespoons soy sauce

Place chicken, skin side up, in large shallow baking pan in single layer. Sprinkle flavor enhancer, salt and pepper on chicken; let stand 10 minutes. Stir together corn oil, honey and soy sauce; drizzle on chicken. Bake, uncovered, in 350° oven, about 1 hour or until fork can be inserted with ease; baste frequently. Makes 4 servings.

1970—Miss Robin Ann Lee, Hamer, South Carolina

Lime imparts a tropical flavor to chicken and brown sugar helps it glaze attractively. The hint of wine in the baking liquid adds to eating pleasure.

CHICKEN IN THE LIMELIGHT

1 broiler-fryer chicken, cut in parts	¼ cup Mazola corn oil
1 lime	2 tablespoons brown sugar
⅓ cup flour	½ cup chicken broth
1½ teaspoons salt	½ cup dry white wine
½ teaspoon paprika	2 sprigs fresh mint (or
1 teaspoon Ac'cent flavor enhancer	½ teaspoon dried mint)

Grate peel from lime and set aside. Squeeze lime juice over pieces of chicken. Mix together flour, salt, paprika and flavor enhancer in bag. Add chicken and shake to coat thoroughly. Heat corn oil in fry pan over medium heat; add chicken and brown on all sides. Place chicken in single layer in shallow baking pan. Mix lime peel and brown sugar; sprinkle over chicken. Add liquids. Place mint on top. Cover and bake in 375° oven approximately 45 minutes, or until fork can be inserted with ease. Garnish with lime wedges, avocado crescents and fresh mint. Makes 4 servings.

1965—Mrs. Janice E. Page, Upton, Massachusetts

You'll be pleased with the delicious corn flake crust on this chicken—and the mellow white grape sauce adds the ideal final touch.

BAKED CHICKEN BREASTS WITH WHITE GRAPE SAUCE

2 whole broiler-fryer chicken breasts, halved, skinned, boned
6 tablespoons flour, divided
1¼ teaspoons salt, divided
1 teaspoon Ac'cent flavor enhancer
½ teaspoon tarragon leaves, crushed
¼ teaspoon pepper

1 egg, beaten
1 tablespoon water
1 cup corn flake crumbs
4 tablespoons Mazola corn oil, divided
1 cup canned chicken broth
4 teaspoons lemon juice
1 cup white grapes
2 egg yolks

Flatten breasts slightly with a food mallet or rolling pin. On a plate, mix ¼ cup of the flour, 1 teaspoon of the salt, flavor enhancer, tarragon and pepper. Mix the egg and water in a small bowl. Place corn flake crumbs in a separate bowl. Line a large shallow baking pan with double thickness of heavy-duty foil. Brush the foil with 1 tablespoon of the corn oil. Dip each breast piece into the seasoned flour and shake off excess. Cover with the egg-water mixture and then dip into the crumbs, coating thoroughly. Place the coated pieces, side by side, in the pan and drizzle 1 tablespoon of the corn oil over the chicken. Refrigerate 1 hour. Bake in a 350° oven 25 minutes, or until fork can be inserted with ease.

To prepare sauce, pour the remaining 2 tablespoons corn oil into a saucepan. Add remaining 2 tablespoons flour and ¼ teaspoon salt. Place over medium heat and blend with a spoon 2 minutes. Gradually stir in chicken broth; continue to stir until sauce thickens. Add lemon juice and white grapes and cook until heated. Remove the saucepan from heat and beat in egg yolks, 1 at a time. Pour the sauce over the chicken. Makes 4 servings.

1973—Mrs. James Hearl (Florence), St. Davids Church, Virginia

If your family likes finger food, you might serve these at dinner. Also a hearty appetizer or midnight snack.

CRUSTY CHICKEN WRAP-UPS

8 broiler-fryer chicken drumsticks
1 teaspoon Ac'cent flavor enhancer
1 teaspoon salt
¼ teaspoon pepper
¼ cup Mazola corn oil
½ cup prepared barbecue sauce

1 package (8 ounces) refrigerated crescent dinner rolls
1 egg, beaten
2 teaspoons grated Parmesan cheese

Sprinkle flavor enhancer, salt and pepper on drumsticks. Heat corn oil in fry pan over medium heat. Add chicken and cook until lightly brown on all sides. Add barbecue sauce; cover and cook, turning occasionally, 25 minutes or until fork can be inserted with ease. Remove pan from heat. Unroll crescent rolls and separate. Brush each triangle with egg and sprinkle with cheese. Place meaty end of drumstick on triangle. Pull dough around chicken and press edges to seal. Place on ungreased baking sheet. Bake in 375° oven about 15 minutes, or until roll is brown. Makes 8 appetizer servings.

1971—Mrs. Thomas Piantek (Gloria), Chicago, Illinois

This is a fine recipe for the cook with a lot to do. The preparation is simple, the finished dish rewarding.

OVEN-FRIED CHICKEN

1 broiler-fryer chicken, cut in parts
¼ cup Mazola corn oil
¼ cup sour cream
1 tablespoon lemon juice
1 teaspoon Worcestershire sauce
1 teaspoon Ac'cent flavor enhancer
1 teaspoon celery salt
1 teaspoon salt
½ teaspoon paprika
1 cup soda cracker crumbs

Mix together all ingredients except chicken and crumbs. Dip pieces of chicken into mixture; then roll in crumbs. Place in a single layer in shallow baking pan and bake in 350° oven for approximately 1 hour, or until fork can be inserted with ease. Makes 4 servings.

1961—Miss Maggie Query, Clover, South Carolina

Dine like a king on this elegant dish. And keep track of the paté recipe—you'll use it often at parties.

PATÉ-STUFFED CHICKEN BREASTS

4 whole broiler-fryer
  chicken breasts, halved,
  boned, skinned
Chicken Liver Paté
  (recipe below)
2 teaspoons Ac'cent flavor
  enhancer

½ cup fine dry breadcrumbs
2 tablespoons grated Par-
  mesan cheese
1 tablespoon paprika
1 egg, slightly beaten

Make paté. Place chicken breasts between sheets of waxed paper and pound thin. Sprinkle each with ¼ teaspoon flavor enhancer and spread with 2 tablespoons paté. Tuck sides in and roll tightly. Fasten with food pick. Mix breadcrumbs, cheese and paprika. Dip breast pieces in beaten egg; roll in crumb mixture. Place chicken rolls in large shallow baking pan, in a single layer. Bake in 350° oven 40 minutes or until fork be inserted with ease. Serve on a bed of rice and top each chicken roll with a dollop of Hollandaise sauce.

Chicken Liver Paté

½ pound broiler-fryer
  chicken livers
¼ cup Mazola corn oil
1 medium onion, chopped
2 tablespoons dry red wine

1 teaspoon Ac'cent flavor
  enhancer
1 teaspoon salt
½ teaspoon pepper

Heat corn oil in a fry pan over medium heat. Saute chicken livers and onion about 5 minutes, or until livers are done. Place wine in blender container. Add contents of fry pan, flavor enhancer, salt and pepper and blend until smooth. Chill. (This may be done days ahead ... it makes a superb cocktail spread.) Makes 8 servings.

1973—Mrs. Charles A. Hauber (Julia), Winfield, Kansas

Although the basic flavors in this recipe are very traditional, the skill with which the bird is seasoned makes this roast chicken outstanding.

ROAST DELMARVA CHICKEN

1 whole broiler-fryer chicken
1 lemon, cut in half
¼ cup pork sausage
¼ cup Mazola corn oil
3 tablespoons chopped onion, divided
½ teaspoon paprika
¼ teaspoon salt
¼ cup chopped celery
¼ cup chopped parsley
4 cups breadcrumbs
½ cup milk
1 teaspoon Ac'cent flavor enhancer
1 teaspoon celery leaves
½ teaspoon crushed rosemary
½ cup cream, divided

Rub skin of chicken with cut lemon and let stand 10 minutes. Cook sausage in fry pan over low heat until golden brown, breaking it into small pieces as it cooks. Reserve 1 tablespoon drippings. Add corn oil and 2 tablespoons of the onion to sausage. Continue cooking until onion is softened, but not browned. Remove pan from heat and add paprika, salt, celery, parsley, breadcrumbs and milk. Stuff the body and neck cavities lightly with sausage mixture. Rub skin with the reserved 1 tablespoon of sausage drippings. Sprinkle flavor enhancer, celery leaves, crushed rosemary and remaining 1 tablespoon onion on outside of chicken. Place chicken on rack in baking pan and cover loosely with foil. Roast at 325° for 45 minutes. Remove foil. Brush with ¼ cup of the cream. Continue baking approximately 20 minutes, basting with remaining cream until brown and leg moves freely when lifted or turned. Garnish with baked halves of oranges, and watercress or parsley. Makes 4 servings.

1952—Mrs. Ernest Schultz, Bordentown, New Jersey

Roast chicken is enhanced with a sweet fruit stuffing—just wait until the children taste it!

HENNY PENNY'S CHICKEN LITTLE

1 whole broiler-fryer
  chicken
1 teaspoon Ac'cent flavor
  enhancer, divided
1 teaspoon salt, divided
½ cup Mazola corn oil
2 cups white bread cubes
  (4 slices cut in ½-inch
  cubes)

1½ cups diced apples
½ cup raisins
2 tablespoons sugar
1 teaspoon cinnamon
1 egg, beaten

Sprinkle ½ teaspoon of the flavor enhancer and ½ teaspoon of the salt on chicken. Heat corn oil in fry pan over medium heat. Add bread cubes and cook, stirring, until brown. Remove pan from heat. Add apples, raisins, sugar, cinnamon and remaining flavor enhancer and salt. Lightly stir in egg. Spoon into cavity of chicken. Hook wing tips onto back and tie legs together. Place in shallow baking pan. Bake, uncovered, in 350° oven about one hour, or until leg moves freely when lifted or turned. Makes 4 servings.

1963—Mrs. V. Houdek, Lake Wales, Florida

Delicate flavorings make this broiled chicken dish very interesting. Perfect accompaniments: buttered asparagus and new potatoes with parsley.

NUTMEG MARINATED CHICKEN

1 broiler-fryer chicken,
  cut in parts
2 lemons, halved
½ cup Mazola corn oil
1 teaspoon Ac'cent flavor
  enhancer
¼ teaspoon ground nutmeg

1 teaspoon salt
¼ teaspoon ground black
  pepper
1 clove garlic, minced
8 large mushrooms,
  quartered

Rub chicken with cut lemon, then squeeze both lemons to make juice. In a saucepan make marinade by mixing together corn oil, flavor enhancer, nutmeg, salt, pepper, garlic and lemon juice and heating for 5 minutes. Place chicken and mushrooms in a flat dish. Pour marinade over, turning to coat all pieces. Marinate, covered, 6 hours or overnight, in a refrigerator. Arrange chicken on foil-lined broiler pan; place pan about 6 inches from heat source and broil 20 minutes on each side, turning as needed. Brush with marinade. Add mushrooms last 10 minutes of cooking period. Makes 4 servings.

1974—Mrs. Robert Bennett (Alice), Coventry, Rhode Island

There's a good chance you'll have all the ingredients on hand for this hearty barbecue sauce which needs no previous cooking.

LAKE MACDONALD CHICKEN GRILLE

2 broiler-fryer chickens, quartered
½ cup Mazola corn oil, divided
½ cup catchup
½ cup cider vinegar
¼ cup beer
2 tablespoons lemon juice
1 tablespoon steak sauce
1 tablespoon soy sauce
1 teaspoon Ac'cent flavor enhancer
¼ teaspoon ground black pepper
¼ teaspoon garlic salt

Brush chicken with ¼ cup of the corn oil; let stand while preparing sauce. Stir together catchup, vinegar, beer, lemon juice, steak sauce, soy sauce, flavor enhancer, pepper, garlic salt and remaining ¼ cup corn oil. Brush chicken with sauce. Arrange chicken on preheated grill about 8 inches from heat source; cook, brushing with sauce every few minutes, turning when partly cooked. Cook 1 hour, or until fork can be inserted with ease. Delicious served outdoors with potato salad, cold beverages, crisp raw vegetables and French bread or hard rolls. Makes 8 servings.

1974—Mr. Clarence C. Lind, Fargo, North Dakota

Mint and rosemary are unusual herbs to find in a barbecue marinade. The flavor's different and very appealing!

PERSIAN CHICKEN KABOBS

4 whole broiler-fryer chicken breasts, halved, boned, skinned, cut into skewer pieces
1 teaspoon Ac'cent flavor enhancer
2 teaspoons salt, divided
¼ cup Mazola corn oil
¼ cup tarragon wine vinegar
½ teaspoon dry mint leaves
¼ teaspoon dry rosemary
1 clove garlic, crushed
¼ teaspoon hot pepper sauce
4 medium tomatoes, quartered
16 small white onions, peeled
2 green peppers, seeded, cut into skewer pieces
16 small to medium fresh mushroom caps

Sprinkle chicken with flavor enhancer and 1 teaspoon of the salt. Mix together corn oil, vinegar, mint, rosemary, garlic and hot pepper sauce. Pour over chicken in flat dish or bowl. Marinate, covered, in refrigerator at least 2 hours or overnight, if possible, turning once or twice. Drain marinade from chicken, reserving marinade to use as brushing sauce. Thread chicken on skewers, alternating with vegetables. Brush with marinade; sprinkle with remaining 1 teaspoon salt. Cook on outdoor grill about 6 inches from heat, turning and basting frequently, 30 minutes or until fork can be inserted with ease. Serve with rice pilaf or plain rice. Makes 6 servings.

1974—Dr. Harold Tara, Wayne, New Jersey

Quite a few ingredients here, but this recipe is nearly a meal in itself. Just add salad and a fantastic dinner is complete!

CHICK KABOBS

6 whole broiler-fryer chicken breasts, boned and skinned
1 can (2 ounces) whole button mushrooms
1 can (7½ ounces) whole white onions

1 large green pepper, cut in one-inch-square pieces
6 skewers
2 tablespoons cornstarch
1 cup water
2 cups cooked rice

Marinade

1 cup catchup
¼ cup Mazola corn oil
1 can (8 ounces) crushed pineapple, not drained
2 tablespoons vinegar
2 tablespoons soy sauce
1 tablespoon lemon juice

¼ cup dried rosemary
2 tablespoons brown sugar
2 teaspoons black pepper
1½ teaspoons salt
1 teaspoon Ac'cent flavor enhancer
1 teaspoon curry powder

Cut each breast into four nuggets about 1½ inches square. Prepare skewers by alternating nuggets with mushrooms, onions and green pepper. Mix together all marinade ingredients. Place prepared skewers in shallow baking dish; pour marinade over. Refrigerate, covered, 4 to 6 hours before cooking.

Place prepared skewers on a preheated charcoal grill 4 inches from the heat. Cook approximately 20 minutes, brushing with marinade and turning until brown and done. Make sauce by mixing cornstarch and water in saucepan and adding remaining marinade. Heat and stir until smooth. Pour most of sauce over hot cooked rice in a deep platter. Lay skewers on rice; pour remaining sauce over kabobs to give a glazed look. Makes 6 servings.

1969—Mrs. Jack O. Wiseman, Searcy, Arkansas

Grilled chicken is enhanced by the fragrance of oranges in a zesty sauce. The orange peel wrapping adds both flavor and visual interest.

ORIENTAL COOK-OUT CHICKEN

2 whole broiler-fryer chickens	½ teaspoon pepper
1 teaspoon salt	2 oranges
1 teaspoon Ac'cent flavor enhancer	

Sauce

1 cup frozen orange juice concentrate, undiluted	2 tablespoons French salad dressing
4 tablespoons Mazola corn oil	3 tablespoons soy sauce

Rub inside of chickens with salt, flavor enhancer and pepper. Make sauce by mixing together ingredients listed. Using pastry brush, brush chicken inside and out with sauce. Peel oranges as apples in long spirals, keeping skins in one strip. Cut orange segments into small pieces and place inside chickens. Tie chickens securely with wings together and tails to legs. Place on charcoal broiler rotisserie rod, securing with forked holders. Place spiral orange peels around chickens, holding in place with food picks. Cook on rotisserie for approximately 1 hour, or until leg moves freely when lifted or turned, basting frequently. Makes 6 to 8 servings.

1967—Mrs. Doris Ekstrom, Clinton, Montana

If a French chef were asked to invent a sophisticated marinade, it would probably be something like this.

CHICKEN OVER-THE-COALS

2 broiler-fryer chickens, quartered
2 cups white wine
1 cup Mazola corn oil
1 cup soy sauce
1 clove garlic, minced
1½ tablespoons lemon juice (juice of ½ lemon)
1 tablespoon freshly ground pepper
2 tablespoons Dijon French mustard
1 teaspoon salt
1 teaspoon Ac'cent flavor enhancer

In a large bowl, mix together all ingredients except chicken to make sauce. Marinate the chicken, covered, at least 2 hours or overnight in sauce. Reserve the marinade. Place chicken quarters on grill, skin side up, about 8 inches from heat. Grill about 1 hour, or until fork can be inserted with ease, turning and brushing with reserved marinade. Makes 8 servings.

1966—Mr. Joel Allard, San Antonio, Texas

Here's a party treat that appeals to every age. Easy-to-eat chicken nuggets with a crunchy sesame-seed crust can be dipped into a choice of three tasty sauces.

"DIPPER'S NUGGETS" CHICKEN

6 whole broiler-fryer chicken breasts, skinned and boned	3 tablespoons sesame seed
2 eggs, beaten	1½ teaspoons salt
1 cup water	1 teaspoon Ac'cent flavor enhancer
1 cup flour	1-1½ pints Mazola corn oil

Cut breast pieces into 1 × 1½-inch nuggets.

Mix eggs and water. Add flour, sesame seed, salt and flavor enhancer to make batter. Heat corn oil in fry pan over medium heat filling utensil no more than ⅓ full. Dip nuggets into batter; drain off excess batter. Add nuggets to oil. Fry about 3 to 5 minutes, or until golden brown and fork can be inserted with ease. Drain on paper towels. Serve with following sauces. Makes 12 servings.

Nippy Pineapple Sauce: In saucepan, mix 1 jar (12 ounces) pineapple preserves, ¼ cup prepared mustard and ¼ cup prepared horseradish. Heat. Makes 1½ cups.

Dill Sauce: In bowl, mix ½ cup sour cream, ½ cup mayonnaise, 1 teaspoon dried dill weed and 2 tablespoons finely chopped dill pickle. Let stand at room temperature for 1 to 2 hours to blend flavors. Makes about ¾ cup.

Royalty Sauce: In saucepan, mix 1 cup catsup, ½ teaspoon dry mustard, 1 tablespoon brown sugar, 2 tablespoons vinegar, 6 tablespoons Mazola margarine. Mix and cook 4 to 5 minutes, stirring constantly. Makes 1 cup.

1971—Mrs. Thomas H. Young, Searcy, Arkansas

This recipe is a lot like chow mein, but there's an exciting difference—red wine! It's a party dish with crowd appeal.

CHINESE CHICKEN LIVERS

2 pounds broiler-fryer chicken livers
2 cups drained bean sprouts
1 cup drained water chestnuts
1 cup drained bamboo shoots
1 cup chopped onion
½ cup chopped green pepper
½ cup soy sauce
1 clove garlic, minced
1 tablespoon Ac'cent flavor enhancer
1 teaspoon pepper
½ teaspoon garlic salt
2 cups red cooking wine
½ cup Mazola corn oil

In a deep mixing bowl, stir together bean sprouts, water chestnuts, bamboo shoots, onion, green pepper, soy sauce, garlic, flavor enhancer, pepper and garlic salt. Pour wine over the ingredients. Cover and chill 2 hours. Heat corn oil in a 5-quart dutch oven over medium heat. Add chicken livers and brown lightly. Drain well. Add the marinated ingredients to the chicken livers in the dutch oven. Cover and cook over low heat 20 minutes, or until done. Serve over brown rice or chow mein noodles. Makes 8 servings.

1973—Ms. Cynthia Gassaway, Tulsa, Oklahoma

Convenience products combine to make a fantastically good casserole. Add mashed potatoes or buttered rice and the meal is complete.

CHICKEN AND ASPARAGUS CASSEROLE

2 whole broiler-fryer chicken breasts, skinned, boned and cut into 2 × 4¾-inch pieces
1½ teaspoons Ac'cent flavor enhancer
¼ teaspoon pepper
½ cup Mazola corn oil
2 packages (10 ounces each) frozen asparagus
1 can condensed cream of chicken soup
½ cup mayonnaise
1 teaspoon lemon juice
½ teaspoon curry powder
1 cup shredded sharp cheddar cheese

Sprinkle flavor enhancer and pepper over chicken. Heat corn oil in a fry pan over medium heat. Add chicken and saute slowly about 6 minutes, or until white and opaque. Remove from fry pan; drain on paper towels. Cook asparagus by package directions 4 to 5 minutes. Drain. Place asparagus on bottom of 9 × 9 × 2-inch baking pan. Place sauteed chicken over asparagus. Mix together chicken soup, mayonnaise, lemon juice and curry powder. Pour over chicken and asparagus. Sprinkle cheese over the top. Cover. Bake in 375° oven 30 minutes, or until fork can be inserted with ease. Makes 4 servings.

1973—Mr. R. Clement Holley, Wilmington, Delaware

HONEY CHICKEN

SWEET 'N SMOKEY CHICKEN

CHEESE DELIGHT IN EVERY BITE CHICKEN

HERB FRIED CHICKEN DRUMSTICKS

HOT CHINESE CHICKEN SALAD

HENNY PENNY'S CHICKEN LITTLE

SWEET AND SOUR CHICKEN

BAKED CHICKEN BREASTS WITH WHITE GRAPE SAUCE

CRUSTY CHICKEN WRAP-UPS

Although you won't find salad recipes in most Chinese cookbooks, this mixture tastes very Oriental. Quick, too!

HOT CHINESE CHICKEN SALAD

8 broiler-fryer chicken
  thighs, skinned, boned,
  cut into 1-inch chunks
¼ cup corn starch
¼ cup Mazola corn oil
⅛ teaspoon garlic powder
1 large ripe tomato, cut
  into chunks
1 can (4 ounces) water
  chestnuts, drained, sliced

1 can (4 ounces) sliced
  mushrooms, drained
1 bunch green onions,
  coarsely chopped
1 cup slant-sliced celery
1 teaspoon Ac'cent flavor
  enhancer
¼ cup soy sauce
2 cups finely shredded
  iceberg lettuce

Roll chicken in corn starch. Heat corn oil in fry pan or wok over high heat. Add chicken chunks and quickly brown. Sprinkle with garlic powder. Add tomato, water chestnuts, mushrooms, onion and celery. Stir. Sprinkle with flavor enhancer. Add soy sauce. Stir. Cover, reduce heat to simmer and cook 5 minutes. Lightly toss chicken-vegetable mix with lettuce. Serve hot with rice. Makes 4 servings.

1974—Mrs. Raymond Lutz (Fayne), Taos, New Mexico

A superb spaghetti dish in which chicken plays a starring role. This one is a great success with children, teens.

CHICKEN TAGGLIARINI

2 whole broiler-fryer chicken breasts, skinned, boned, cut in ½-inch strips
1 teaspoon Ac'cent flavor enhancer
¼ cup Mazola corn oil
2 medium onions, chopped
2 cloves garlic, minced
1 teaspoon chili powder
1 can (16 ounces) whole kernel corn, undrained
1 cup small ripe olives, pitted
1 can (4 ounces) tomato paste
1 can (8 ounces) tomato sauce
12 ounces thin spaghetti
1 cup grated sharp cheddar cheese

Sprinkle chicken with flavor enhancer. Heat corn oil in fry pan over medium heat. Saute chicken, onions and garlic about 6 minutes. Add chili powder, corn, olives, tomato paste and tomato sauce. Mix well. Simmer while preparing spaghetti according to package directions. Place drained spaghetti in greased flat baking dish. Add chicken medley; sprinkle with cheese. Bake in 350° oven 15 minutes, or until fork can be inserted with ease and cheese is bubbly. Makes 8 servings.

1974—Mrs. Basil Sweet (Lois), Lafayette, Indiana

PART IV
1975 Winners
National Chicken
Cooking Contest

Alabama

Two basting mixtures distinguish this barbecued chicken recipe. The first adds deep-down flavor, the second, a sunny glazing.

HONEY BARBECUED CHICKEN

2 broiler-fryer chickens, halved
¾ cup wine vinegar
¼ cup Mazola corn oil
1 teaspoon Ac'cent flavor enhancer
1 teaspoon garlic salt
1 teaspoon ground cayenne pepper
1 teaspoon paprika
¼ teaspoon hot pepper sauce
¾ cup bottled barbecue sauce
2 tablespoons honey

In a bowl stir together vinegar, corn oil, flavor enhancer, garlic salt, cayenne pepper, paprika and hot pepper sauce. Place chicken on grill, skin side up, about 8 inches from heat. Cook, turning and basting with sauce mixture approximately 1 hour or until leg moves freely when lifted or turned. Spread barbecue sauce and honey over chicken; turn and baste all sides. Cook about 5 minutes after adding honey. Chicken may be served hot or cold. Makes 4 servings.

Dr. T. Dewey Harden, Jr., Enterprise, Alabama

Alaska

Here's the popular combination of peanut butter and bacon used to bring an exciting new taste to chicken breasts.

PLANTATION CHICKEN ROLLS

4 whole broiler-fryer chicken breasts, halved, boned and skinned

2 teaspoons Ac'cent flavor enhancer

½ cup creamy peanut butter

½ pound bacon, crisply cooked, drained, crumbled

¼ cup flour

1½ teaspoons salt

2 eggs, well beaten

1½ cups fine dry bread-crumbs

⅓ cup Mazola corn oil

Place chicken between 2 sheets of waxed paper and flatten with mallet or knife handle to ¼" thickness. Sprinkle with flavor enhancer. Spread each with about 1 tablespoon peanut butter; then sprinkle on each about 1 tablespoon crumbled bacon. Fold edges in and roll; secure with a wooden pick. Mix flour and salt; coat rolls lightly. Dip in egg then coat with breadcrumbs. Heat corn oil in fry pan over medium heat. Add chicken and brown on all sides. Reduce heat and cover; cook over medium-low heat, turning as needed, about 40 minutes or until fork can be inserted with ease. Remove picks. Serve with spiced apple rings or small cups apple jelly. Makes 8 servings.

Ms. Patricia Whittlesey, Petersburg, Alaska

Arizona

Many very fine cooks substitute frozen puff pastry shells for their own homemade pastry. Try the following recipe and find out what elegance they lend to chicken.

CHICKEN PUFFS

3 whole broiler-fryer chicken breasts, halved, boned and skinned
¼ cup Mazola corn oil
1 teaspoon Ac'cent flavor enhancer
½ teaspoon salt
¼ teaspoon dried rosemary leaves

1 package (10 ounces) frozen puff pastry party shells, partly thawed
1 package (3 ounces) cream cheese with chives, cut in 6 pieces

Heat corn oil in fry pan over medium heat. Add chicken and brown on all sides. While cooking, sprinkle with flavor enhancer, salt and rosemary. Roll each pastry shell to a circle about 9 inches in diameter. Place a chicken breast on ½ of each pastry circle. (If necessary, cut chicken to fit.) Spread each piece of chicken with 1 piece of chive cheese. Fold pastry over chicken and seal edges. Place chicken filled pastry on baking sheet. Place in 450° oven; immediately reduce temperature to 400°. Bake, uncovered, about 30 minutes or until golden brown and fork can be inserted with ease. Makes 6 servings.

Mrs. Harry Hofford (Anne), Phoenix, Arizona

Arkansas

Delicious fried chicken with an unusual broiled topping. Final touch—a piquant sauce. Party pretty!

CHICKEN VIENNESE

4 whole broiler-fryer chicken breasts, halved, boned, skinned and flattened to ½-inch
1 teaspoon salt
1 teaspoon Ac'cent flavor enhancer
¼ teaspoon pepper
1 egg
¼ cup water
⅓ cup flour
1 cup fine dry breadcrumbs
½ cup Mazola corn oil
8 thin slices Swiss cheese, cut to fit chicken pieces
8 thin slices ham
8 pineapple rings, drained
½ cup margarine
2 teaspoons prepared mustard
2 tablespoons lemon juice

Sprinkle chicken with salt, flavor enhancer and pepper. Beat egg and water. Dredge chicken with flour; dip into egg-water mixture. Coat with breadcrumbs. Heat corn oil in large fry pan over medium heat. Add chicken and cook approximately 10-15 minutes each side or until fork can be inserted with ease and chicken is brown. Remove and drain. Place chicken in single layer on broiler pan. Place a slice of cheese, then ham and top with pineapple slice on each piece. Broil about 6 inches from heat until cheese melts a bit. In a small saucepan melt margarine over medium heat. Stir in mustard and lemon juice; keep warm. Garnish platter with lemon slices and parsley; spoon sauce over each serving. Makes 8 servings.

Mrs. Rollin L. Richardson (Patricia), Little Rock, Arkansas

California

Here's a dish which combines vegetable *and* fruit flavors with a zesty *and* sweet sauce. Eating fun, winter or summer.

FRUIT 'N' CHICKEN KABOBS

2 whole broiler-fryer chicken breasts, halved, boned, skinned and cut in 1½-inch pieces
¼ cup Mazola corn oil
2 tablespoons lemon juice
1 teaspoon Ac'cent flavor enhancer
½ teaspoon salt
⅛ teaspoon pepper
12 canned pineapple chunks
3 oranges, each cut into 4 wedges
12 cherry tomatoes
1 large green pepper, seeded, cut in chunks
¼ cup bottled barbecue sauce
1 jar (12 ounces) pineapple preserves

Mix together corn oil and lemon juice. Pour over chicken and marinate 1 hour. Drain and reserve marinade. Sprinkle chicken with flavor enhancer, salt and pepper. Spear chicken chunks alternately with pineapple, tomatoes, pepper and orange. In small saucepan mix together reserved marinade, barbecue sauce and preserves. Heat, stirring constantly, until mixture is blended. Brush kabobs generously. Place on broiler rack and broil about 3 inches from heat about 5 minutes. Turn and brush with preserve mixture. Broil about 5 minutes longer, or until fork can be inserted with ease. Makes 4 servings.

Mrs. Mary G. Cerami, Ojai, California

Colorado

Contrasts in flavor—sweet and tart, prunes and onion—give this baked chicken dish a Victorian elegance.

GOURMET GLAZED CHICKEN

8 broiler-fryer chicken thighs
¼ cup flour
¼ cup Mazola corn oil
⅓ cup plum jelly
¼ cup port wine
3 tablespoons lemon juice
1 teaspoon Ac'cent flavor enhancer
¾ teaspoon salt
¼ teaspoon grated lemon rind
1 cup pitted prunes
½ cup thinly sliced onion

Coat chicken in flour. Heat corn oil in fry pan over medium heat. Add chicken and brown on all sides. Place chicken in single layer, skin side up, in large shallow baking pan. Stir together jelly, wine, lemon juice, flavor enhancer, salt and lemon rind. Pour over chicken. Scatter prunes and onion slices over top. Cover with foil. Bake in 400° oven about 30 minutes. Remove foil and bake, basting twice, about 10 minutes or until fork can be inserted with ease. Makes 4 servings.

Mrs. Marlene M. Buck, Littleton, Colorado

Connecticut

Here's a recipe on the sweet side, crunchy with walnuts, fragrant with fruit. An excellent main dish for a crowd.

ORANGE-BANANA GLAZED CHICKEN BREASTS

6 whole broiler-fryer chicken breasts, boned
1 teaspoon Ac'cent flavor enhancer
2½ cups soft breadcrumbs
1 cup chopped walnuts
⅓ cup Mazola corn oil
2 medium-ripe bananas
½ cup frozen concentrated orange juice, thawed
2 tablespoons lemon juice
½ cup dark corn syrup

Sprinkle chicken with flavor enhancer. Lay breasts, skin side down, in a well greased large shallow baking pan. Mix together crumbs, walnuts and corn oil. Spoon equal portions breadcrumb mixture on one half each breast; fold over the other half and skewer the edges together. Peel and mash bananas. Stir in orange juice, lemon juice and corn syrup. Brush all of mixture on chicken. Bake, uncovered, in a 375° oven about 1 hour, basting every 15 minutes, until fork can be inserted with ease. When ready to serve, remove skewers and cut each breast in half. Makes 12 servings.

Ms. Marion Dunnell, Hartford, Connecticut

Delaware

Like many Polynesian recipes, this dish is both fruity and zesty, with a garnish which adds flavor accent.

CHICKEN TUTTI-FRUITI

4 whole broiler-fryer chicken breasts, halved and skinned
½ cup Mazola corn oil
1 teaspoon lemon-pepper seasoning
1 can (16 ounces) crushed pineapple
1 cup orange juice
2 tablespoons brown sugar
2 teaspoons Ac'cent flavor enhancer
2 teaspoons soy sauce
1 teaspoon salt

Heat corn oil in fry pan over medium heat. Add chicken and brown on all sides. Sprinkle with lemon-pepper seasoning. Cover and simmer 20 minutes. In a bowl mix together pineapple, orange juice, brown sugar, flavor enhancer, soy sauce and salt. Spoon over chicken. Cook, covered, over low heat about 40 minutes or until fork can be inserted with ease. Garnish with green grapes and maraschino cherries. Makes 8 servings.

Mrs. James E. Johnson (Edith), Wilmington, Delaware

District of Columbia

This European classic tastes better than ever when chicken is the prime ingredient. Elegant but hearty.

CHICKEN PAPRIKASH

2 whole broiler-fryer chicken breasts, halved
4 broiler-fryer chicken thighs
4 broiler-fryer chicken drumsticks
1 teaspoon Ac'cent flavor enhancer
¼ cup Mazola corn oil
4 medium onions, finely chopped
2 tablespoons paprika
2 green peppers, seeded, thinly sliced
2 tomatoes, thinly sliced
¼ pound mushroom caps
½ cup chicken broth
1 teaspoon salt
¼ teaspoon pepper
1½ cups dairy sour cream
1 tablespoon flour

Sprinkle chicken with flavor enhancer. Heat corn oil in large fry pan over medium heat. Add onions and saute until clear. Remove fry pan from direct heat and stir in paprika. Return to heat; add chicken and cook gently about 10 minutes per side to coat chicken with onions and paprika. Drain off excess fat. Add peppers, tomatoes, mushrooms, chicken broth, salt and pepper. Simmer, covered, on low heat about 45 minutes or until fork can be inserted with ease. Blend sour cream and flour. Remove chicken to platter; keep warm. Add sour cream mixture to sauce in fry pan and bring to simmer, stirring constantly. Pour sauce over chicken. Makes 6 servings.

Ms. Jane W. Schweiker, Washington, D.C.

Florida

If you dislike cooking on a summer Sunday, prepare the following on Saturday for later enjoyment. Uncooked sauerkraut is an unusual ingredient.

ZIPPY SUNDAY CHICKEN SALAD

---

2 whole broiler-fryer chicken breasts, halved, skinned
4 broiler-fryer chicken thighs, skinned
¾ cup sugar
½ cup Mazola corn oil, divided
3 tablespoons vinegar

1 cup chopped celery
1 cup chopped green pepper
½ cup toasted slivered almonds
1 teaspoon Ac'cent flavor enhancer
1 can (16 ounces) sauerkraut, drained

In small saucepan make dressing by mixing together sugar, ¼ cup of the corn oil and vinegar. Heat, stirring constantly, until sugar is dissolved. Cool. Heat remaining corn oil in fry pan over medium heat. Add chicken and brown lightly on all sides. Cover; reduce heat. Simmer about 45 minutes or until fork can be inserted with ease. Cool; separate meat from bones and cut in bite-size pieces. In a large bowl place chicken, celery, green pepper, almonds and flavor enhancer. Mix well. Add sauerkraut and corn oil-vinegar dressing. Chill in refrigerator a few hours or overnight. Makes 6 servings.

Ms. Catherine Selby, Christmas, Florida

Georgia

Self-rising flour and a rich chicken flavor give this fried chicken Southern individuality. Good served with creamy cole slaw.

CHILI CHICKEN

1 whole broiler-fryer
chicken, cut in parts
1 egg
½ cup milk
1 cup self-rising flour

1 envelope (1¾ ounces)
chili seasoning mix
2 teaspoons Ac'cent flavor
enhancer
1 cup Mazola corn oil

With fork beat egg and milk. In bowl mix together flour, seasoning mix and flavor enhancer. Dip chicken in egg; then in flour mixture. Heat corn oil in fry pan over medium heat. Add chicken and brown on all sides. Reduce heat. Cover and cook about 45 minutes or until fork can be inserted with ease. Drain. Serve hot or cold. Makes 4 servings.

Ms. Dorene C. Sudweeks, Griffin, Georgia

Hawaii

Tempura is a Japanese classic—this is an easy-to-make American version.

CHICKEN TEMPURA

2 whole broiler-fryer chicken breasts, halved, boned, skinned, and cut in 1-inch cubes, flattened
1 teaspoon Ac'cent flavor enhancer
1 teaspoon salt, divided
1 tablespoon catchup
1 tablespoon soy sauce

2 eggs
¾ cup water
½ cup flour
½ cup corn starch
1 quart (about) Mazola corn oil
1 recipe Soy Sauce Dip
1 recipe Catchup Dip

Place chicken in bowl and sprinkle on flavor enhancer, ½ teaspoon of the salt; pour on catchup and soy sauce. Marinate about 30 minutes. Beat eggs with water; add flour, corn starch and remaining salt. Stir just until mixed. Dip chicken pieces in batter. Heat corn oil in deep fryer, filling utensil no more than ⅓ full, to 375°. Carefully place chicken, a small amount at a time, in hot corn oil. Turn and cook until light brown. Drain on paper towels. Serve while hot with choice of dips. Makes 4 servings.

SOY SAUCE DIP: In small bowl stir together ⅓ cup soy sauce, 1 tablespoon dry mustard and 1 tablespoon grated turnip.

CATCHUP DIP: Stir ¼ cup catchup and 1 tablespoon sweet relish together.

Mrs. Kiyoko H. Aoki, Honolulu, Hawaii

Idaho

An open-face sandwich can make a distinguished entree when served with green vegetables and a salad. By itself, the recipe makes a fine brunch or luncheon entree.

CHICKEN 'N' SWISS EXTRAORDINAIRE

3 whole broiler-fryer
   chicken breasts, halved,
   skinned and boned
1 teaspoon Ac'cent flavor
   enhancer
½ cup flour
¼ cup Mazola corn oil

6 thick slices French bread
6 slices Swiss cheese
1 tablespoon butter
½ pound mushrooms, sliced
⅔ cup white wine
1 teaspoon salt
¼ teaspoon pepper

Sprinkle chicken with flavor enhancer. Roll in flour. Heat corn oil in fry pan over medium heat. Add chicken and brown on all sides. Reduce heat; cover tightly and cook about 10 minutes or until fork can be inserted with ease. Place bread topped with cheese slices on baking sheet. Heat in 200° oven while preparing mushrooms. Remove chicken from fry pan. Add butter to fry pan; add mushrooms and saute over low heat about 3 minutes. Push mushrooms aside; add wine and stir to loosen browned bits. Add salt and pepper. Return chicken to fry pan and simmer until sauce is slightly thickened. (Sauce may be thickened with a bit of flour if desired.) Place chicken piece on top of each bread slice and spoon mushrooms and sauce over chicken. Makes 6 servings.

Mrs. Floyd W. Graefe (Caroline), Council, Idaho

Illinois

This recipe combines several time-tested ideas—a buttermilk dip, a corn flake crust and a marmalade basting—into one unique recipe. Home-style!

MANDARIN CHICKEN

1 broiler-fryer chicken, cut in parts
2 cups crushed corn flakes
2 teaspoons Ac'cent flavor enhancer
1 tablespoon seasoned salt

1½ cups buttermilk
1 jar (8 ounces) orange marmalade
¼ cup Mazola corn oil
2 teaspoons corn starch

Mix together corn flake crumbs, flavor enhancer and seasoned salt. Dip chicken in buttermilk and then into crumb mixture. Place chicken skin side up in single layer in large shallow baking pan. In a saucepan mix marmalade, corn oil and corn starch. Bring to boil, stirring frequently. Spoon over chicken. Bake in 350° oven about 1¼ hours or until fork can be inserted with ease. Makes 4 servings.

Mrs. Thomas W. Bradley (Gloria), Naperville, Illinois

Indiana

Subtle flavorings distinguish this simple dish with celery contributing its fine, clear essence.

CHICKEN WITH SOUR CREAM AND CELERY

6 broiler-fryer chicken thighs
1½ teaspoons sesame seed
½ teaspoon celery seed
½ tablespoon paprika
¼ teaspoon salt
⅟₁₆ teaspoon garlic powder
⅟₁₆ teaspoon pepper
¼ cup Mazola corn oil
½ cup white wine
1 tablespoon lemon juice
1 red onion, thinly sliced
1 teaspoon Ac'cent flavor enhancer
10 celery stalks, quartered
½ pint dairy sour cream

Mix together sesame seed, celery seed, paprika, salt, garlic powder and pepper. Heat corn oil in large fry pan over medium heat. Add chicken and brown on all sides. Sprinkle ½ of the seasoning mixture on each side of chicken while browning. Drain off fat. Add wine, lemon juice, onion, flavor enhancer and celery. Reduce heat. Cook, covered, about 20 minutes or until fork can be inserted with ease. Remove chicken and celery to serving platter. Slowly add sour cream to sauce in fry pan; mix well and heat, pour sauce over chicken. Makes 6 servings.

Mr. Tom Burnison, Bloomington, Indiana

Iowa

The marinade for this chicken recipe gives it a very unusual taste. A different fried chicken!

CHICKEN U.S.A. PRIMITIVE

2 broiler-fryer chickens, cut in parts
1 cup evaporated milk, undiluted
¼ cup cider vinegar
2 cloves garlic, crushed
1 cup cornmeal
¼ cup corn starch

2 teaspoons Ac'cent flavor enhancer
1 teaspoon salt
1 teaspoon paprika
½ teaspoon freshly ground black pepper
¼ cup Mazola corn oil

In a bowl stir together milk, vinegar and garlic. Add chicken and let stand, turning occasionally, refrigerated at least 4 hours. In a pie plate mix together cornmeal, corn starch, flavor enhancer, salt, paprika and pepper. Drain marinated chicken; roll in meal mixture until well coated. Heat corn oil in fry pan over medium heat. Add chicken and brown on all sides. Lower heat and cook chicken, uncovered, turning frequently, about 35 minutes or until fork can be inserted with ease. Makes 8 servings.

Mrs. Mary Davis, West Des Moines, Iowa

Kansas

The ingredients are tried-and-true favorites and the balance of tastes just right. An easy dish for family or friends.

FUNKY CHICKEN

1 broiler-fryer chicken, cut in parts
½ cup flour
¼ teaspoon salt
¼ teaspoon pepper
¼ teaspoon garlic salt
1 cup Mazola corn oil
1 cup apricot preserves
½ cup bottled barbecue sauce
2 tablespoons soy sauce
1 teaspoon Ac'cent flavor enhancer
1 small onion, chopped

In a pie plate mix together flour, salt, pepper and garlic salt. Coat chicken. Heat corn oil in fry pan over medium heat. Add chicken and brown on all sides. Mix together preserves, barbecue sauce, soy sauce, flavor enhancer and onion. Place chicken in single layer, skin side up, in large shallow baking pan. Pour sauce over chicken. Cover with foil. Bake in 350° oven about 1 hour or until fork can be inserted with ease. Makes 4 servings.

Mrs. Kenton W. Casad (Bea), Stockton, Kansas

Kentucky

Many people like fruit and chicken combination—this recipe features no less than three fruit flavors.

APRICOT CHICKEN REGAL

1 broiler-fryer chicken, cut in parts
1 teaspoon salt
¼ cup Mazola corn oil
1 tablespoon sugar
4 teaspoons corn starch
1 can (30 ounces) apricots, drained, juice reserved
⅔ cup orange juice
⅔ cup apple juice
½ teaspoon whole cloves
1 teaspoon Ac'cent flavor enhancer
1 stick (2 inches) cinnamon
2 teaspoons soy sauce

Sprinkle chicken with salt. Heat corn oil in fry pan over medium heat. Add chicken and brown on all sides. In a saucepan stir together sugar, corn starch, 1 cup reserved apricot juice, orange juice, apple juice, cloves, flavor enhancer and cinnamon. Cook over medium heat, stirring constantly, until mixture thickens; boil about 1 minute. Stir in soy sauce. Remove chicken from fry pan; drain off most of the fat. Add the fruit juice mixture to the drippings and stir to blend. Return chicken to fry pan and simmer, uncovered, about 30 minutes. Turn chicken, add the apricots and cook about 30 minutes longer or until fork can be inserted in chicken with ease. Serve with rice, spooning sauce over rice. Makes 4 servings.

Mrs. E. V. Welty (Violet), Paducah, Kentucky

Louisiana

This chicken bakes in three stages—first, to brown; second, to flavor deeply with fruity wine sauce; finally to complete browning under a parsley-mushroom topping.

POULET DES PÊCHES AU VIN (CHICKEN WITH PEACHES AND WINE)

5 whole broiler-fryer chicken breasts, halved
2 tablespoons paprika
4 teaspoons salt
1 teaspoon Ac'cent flavor enhancer
½ teaspoon dried rosemary leaves
½ teaspoon dried thyme leaves
½ teaspoon black pepper
¼ teaspoon cayenne pepper
⅓ cup Mazola corn oil

1 teaspoon bottled browning sauce
1 jar (29 ounces) spiced peaches, drained, ¾ cup juice reserved
¼ cup lemon juice
1 cup dry vermouth, divided
3 tablespoons dry sherry wine
1 can (4 ounces) sliced mushrooms
½ cup chopped parsley

Mix together paprika, salt, flavor enhancer, rosemary, thyme and pepper. Sprinkle on chicken. Place corn oil and browning sauce in a large shallow baking pan. Add chicken skin side up. Cover loosely with foil. Bake, in 425° oven, turning chicken occasionally, approximately 20-25 minutes or until chicken is browned. Mix together reserved peach juice, lemon juice, ½ cup of the vermouth and sherry wine. Pour mixture on chicken. Reduce heat to 325°. Cover and continue baking about 1 hour or until fork can be inserted with ease. Remove cover, add mushrooms and parsley and remaining ½ cup vermouth. Bake, uncovered, about 10 minutes. Garnish platter with peaches and parsley. Makes 10 servings.

Ms. Shirley Fay Toups, Baton Rouge, Louisiana

Maine

Notice that the chicken is simmered before it is browned—
one way to insure perfect doneness. The sauce adds melt-in-
your-mouth flavor.

HUBBY'S FAVORITE
SAUCY CHICKEN

- 2 whole broiler-fryer chicken breasts, halved
- 4 broiler-fryer chicken thighs
- 2 cups boiling water
- 1 large onion, divided
- 2 celery stalks with leaves, cut in 2-inch pieces
- 2½ teaspoons Ac'cent flavor enhancer, divided
- 2 teaspoons salt, divided
- ½ teaspoon pepper
- ½ cup Mazola corn oil, divided
- ½ cup catchup
- ¼ cup water
- 1 tablespoon brown sugar
- 2 tablespoons vinegar
- 1 teaspoon dry mustard
- ½ teaspoon garlic powder
- ¼ teaspoon hot pepper sauce

In a large saucepan place chicken, boiling water, 1 slice
of the onion, celery, 1 teaspoon each of the flavor enhancer
and salt, and pepper. Cover. Simmer gently about 30 minutes
or until fork can be inserted with ease. Remove chicken and
drain. Heat ¼ cup of the corn oil in a fry pan over medium
heat. Add chicken and brown lightly on all sides. Chop remaining onion. In a saucepan stir together remaining corn
oil, chopped onion, flavor enhancer and salt. Stir in catchup,
water, brown sugar, vinegar, dry mustard, garlic powder and
pepper sauce. Bring to boil over medium heat. Spoon about
½ the hot sauce over chicken in fry pan. Cook, uncovered,
over medium heat about 10 minutes. Turn chicken; add remaining sauce and cook, uncovered, about 25 minutes. Makes
6 servings.

Mrs. Lawrence E. Hoyt (Ernestine), Fairfield, Maine

Maryland

Chicken and ham are natural flavor partners. In this roll-up recipe, deviled ham makes a hearty filling.

CHICKEN ROLLS

2 whole broiler-fryer chicken breasts, halved, boned and skinned
1 teaspoon Ac'cent flavor enhancer
1 can (2 ounces) deviled ham
¼ cup soft breadcrumbs
1 teaspoon Worcestershire sauce

1 teaspoon minced onion
½ teaspoon salt
¼ teaspoon pepper
¼ teaspoon dry mustard
⅓ cup flour
½ cup Mazola corn oil
1 can (10¾ ounces) cream of mushroom soup

Sprinkle chicken with flavor enhancer. Place on surface, smooth side down. In a bowl stir together deviled ham, breadcrumbs, Worcestershire sauce, onion, salt, pepper and dry mustard. Place about ¼ the filling on each piece chicken. Roll as for jelly roll; secure with wooden picks. Coat rolls with flour. Heat corn oil in fry pan over medium heat. Add chicken and brown on all sides. Place rolls in single layer in large shallow baking pan. Pour soup over chicken. Bake in 350° oven, covered, 20 minutes; remove cover and bake 10 minutes longer or until fork can be inserted with ease. Makes 4 servings.

Mrs. Calvin C. Majerle (Joan), Bowie, Maryland

Massachusetts

If you like natural flavors, you'll welcome this recipe. Sunflower seeds and brown rice help make the unusual stuffing.

BONELESS CHICKEN BREASTS
WITH BROWN RICE STUFFING

4 whole broiler-fryer chicken breasts, boned and skinned
1 teaspoon Ac'cent flavor enhancer
1 teaspoon salt
¼ teaspoon pepper

Brown Rice Stuffing
½ cup sherry wine
3 tablespoons soy sauce
¼ teaspoon paprika
2 scallions, chopped (include green tops)

Sprinkle chicken with flavor enhancer, salt and pepper. Place pieces on flat surface and flatten out. Place about ¼ cup Brown Rice Stuffing on each piece. Roll and secure with wooden picks. Place side by side in single layer in large shallow baking pan. Mix sherry and soy sauce; baste generously. Sprinkle with paprika. Basting frequently, bake in 350° oven about 30 minutes, or until a fork can be inserted with ease. Remove chicken; keep warm. Place pan with drippings on range over medium heat. Add remaining basting mixture and cook 3 minutes. Toss in scallions, cook 30 seconds. Pour sauce over chicken and serve with extra stuffing. Makes 4 servings.

BROWN RICE STUFFING

1 cup brown rice
¼ cup Mazola corn oil
1 medium onion, chopped
1 cup hulled raw sunflower seeds
¼ teaspoon sage
¼ teaspoon thyme
¼ teaspoon marjoram
2 tablespoons soy sauce
½ cup water

Cook rice according to package directions. Heat corn oil in fry pan. Add onion and cook until translucent. Add sunflower seeds and cook 1 minute to brown. Add rest of ingredients. Stir and simmer about 15 minutes. Add cooked rice and toss to mix well.

Ms. Anne Lipman, Brookline, Massachusetts

Michigan

This is a carefully thought out recipe that should please every diner. Inspired by Indian-style cooking, but all-American good!

CYNTHIA'S COUNTRY CAPTAIN CHICKEN

1 broiler-fryer chicken, cut in parts, skinned
2 cups orange marmalade
⅓ cup prepared mustard
¼ cup Mazola corn oil
1½ teaspoons curry powder
1 teaspoon Ac'cent flavor enhancer
½ teaspoon salt
2 tablespoons lemon juice
1 lemon, thinly sliced, seeded
2 tablespoons corn starch
½ cup chicken broth

Place chicken in single layer in large shallow baking pan. In saucepan mix together marmalade, mustard, corn oil, curry powder, flavor enhancer and salt. Cook over medium heat, stirring constantly, until well blended. Add lemon juice; pour over chicken. Cover with foil. Bake in 375° oven, covered, about 45 minutes. Remove cover; baste. Top with lemon slices. Bake 30 minutes longer or until fork can be inserted with ease. Remove to serving platter. Pour drippings into saucepan. Mix corn starch and chicken broth; stir into mixture over medium heat. Cook, stirring constantly, until thickened. Pour over chicken. Makes 4 servings.

Mrs. Cynthia DeFilippo, Detroit, Michigan

Minnesota

This recipe might have been invented in Berlin (instead of Minnesota). Serve with mashed potatoes or buttered noodles, and a nutritious meal is complete.

CHICKEN 'N' KRAUT

8 broiler-fryer chicken thighs
1 teaspoon Ac'cent flavor enhancer
½ teaspoon salt
¼ cup Mazola corn oil
½ cup chopped onion
1 can (1 pound, 11 ounces) sauerkraut, drained
¼ cup water
1 tablespoon caraway seeds
¼ cup packed brown sugar
1 cooking apple, cored, sliced

Sprinkle chicken with flavor enhancer and salt. Heat corn oil in fry pan over medium heat. Add chicken and brown on all sides. Add onion and cook until onion is tender. Add sauerkraut, water, caraway seeds and brown sugar; mix well. Cook, covered, about 10 minutes. Add apple slices and cook about 20 minutes or until fork can be inserted in chicken with ease. Makes 4 servings.

Mrs. Lloyd A. Roczniak (Jean), Rochester, Minnesota

Mississippi

Put together ordinary ingredients like tomato soup and canned mushrooms in an extraordinary way and you'll come up with a dish with prize-winning flavor.

CHICKEN PAPRIKA

2 whole broiler-fryer chicken breasts, halved
2 broiler-fryer chicken thighs
2 broiler-fryer chicken drumsticks
1½ teaspoons Ac'cent flavor enhancer
⅓ cup flour
1 teaspoon salt
¼ teaspoon pepper
⅓ cup Mazola corn oil
2 cans (10½ ounces each) tomato soup
2 cans (4 ounces each) sliced mushrooms, drained
½ cup water
½ cup chopped onion
1 tablespoon paprika
1 large bay leaf
1 cup sour cream

Sprinkle chicken with flavor enhancer. Mix together flour, salt and pepper. Roll chicken in flour to coat. Heat corn oil in fry pan over medium heat. Add chicken and brown on all sides. Pour off excess fat. Add tomato soup, mushrooms, water, onion, paprika and bay leaf. Stir. Simmer, covered, 45 minutes or until a fork can be inserted with ease. Stir now and then. Remove bay leaf. Blend in sour cream; heat. Serve with noodles. Makes 8 servings.

Mrs. John P. Pouncey (Eloyse), Gautier, Mississippi

Missouri

Chicken livers—healthful and delicious—make a tasty filling for these chicken rolls simmered in winey brown gravy.

SHERRIED CHICKEN ROLLS

4 whole broiler-fryer chicken breasts, halved, boned and skinned
1 teaspoon Ac'cent flavor enhancer
¼ pound chicken livers, cooked
¼ cup seedless raisins
2 green onions, finely chopped (tops included)
½ cup soft breadcrumbs
¼ teaspoon garlic powder
1 can (4 ounces) mushroom bits and pieces, undrained, divided
1 egg, beaten
¼ cup Mazola corn oil
1 cup dry sherry wine
1 package (¾ ounce) brown gravy mix

Gently flatten chicken breasts between pieces of waxed paper; sprinkle with flavor enhancer. Mince chicken livers discarding any veiny parts. Mix together chicken livers, raisins, onions, breadcrumbs, garlic powder, 2 tablespoons of the mushroom and egg. Place about 2 tablespoons liver mixture on each breast; roll and fasten with food picks or skewers. Heat corn oil in large fry pan over medium heat and brown chicken on all sides. Mix together sherry, gravy mix, remainder of mushrooms and mushroom liquid. Pour over chicken in fry pan and stir gently until gravy thickens. Cover tightly and simmer gently about 1 hour or until fork can be inserted with ease, adding water occasionally if necessary. Remove food picks and place chicken on serving platter; pour sauce over it. Makes 8 servings.

Mrs. Peggy Creed, Florissant, Missouri

Montana

Three Bean Salad is an American favorite for buffets, luncheons and summer salads. With chicken added, it becomes a new main dish.

CHICKEN THREE BEAN SALAD

2 whole broiler-fryer chicken breasts, simmered, skinned, boned, cut in small pieces
1 can (16 ounces) green beans, drained
1 can (16 ounces) yellow beans, drained
1 can (16 ounces) kidney beans, drained, rinsed
½ cup chopped onion
¼ cup chopped green pepper
¾ cup Mazola corn oil
½ cup cider vinegar
4 tablespoons sugar
2 teaspoons Ac'cent flavor enhancer
1 teaspoon salt
¼ teaspoon pepper

In a large bowl place green beans, yellow beans, kidney beans, onion, green pepper and chicken; mix. In a jar mix corn oil, vinegar, sugar, flavor enhancer, salt and pepper. Pour over chicken-bean mixture; stir to mix well. Cover; refrigerate, stirring occasionally, at least 10 hours or overnight. Makes 6 servings.

SIMMERED CHICKEN: Place 2 whole broiler-fryer chicken breasts in kettle with 2 cups water. Add 1 teaspoon salt and ¼ teaspoon pepper. Bring to boil; cover tightly. Reduce heat and simmer 45 minutes or until a fork can be inserted with ease. Remove from heat; strain broth. Refrigerate chicken and broth. (Reserve broth for later use.)

Mrs. Fred Wilson, Jr. (Donna Sue), Wilsall, Montana

Nebraska

The last-minute addition of marmalade and sesame seeds give this recipe for boned chicken thighs distinctive character. Family fare!

GLAZED SESAME CHICKEN

8 broiler-fryer chicken thighs
¼ cup Mazola corn oil
1 teaspoon Ac'cent flavor enhancer
½ teaspoon onion salt
½ cup orange marmalade
¼ cup sesame seed

Brush chicken with corn oil on all sides. Mix flavor enhancer and salt; sprinkle on all sides. Place on rack in broiler pan on lowest rack in broiler. Broil about 20 minutes, basting with corn oil once or twice. Turn and broil about 20 minutes on second side. Spread marmalade on chicken; sprinkle with sesame seed. Broil about 5 minutes watching carefully. Turn; spread with marmalade, sprinkle with sesame seed. Broil about 5 minutes longer or until fork can be inserted with ease. Makes 4 servings.

Mrs. Ann Berreth, Lincoln, Nebraska

Nevada

The flavors of this recipe will remind you of the best French onion soup you ever tasted. A surprising baking sauce for versatile chicken.

CHICKEN FRENCH ONION CASSEROLE

2 whole broiler-fryer chicken breasts, halved, skinned
4 broiler-fryer chicken thighs, skinned
¼ cup Mazola corn oil
4 medium onions, sliced
1 tablespoon flour
1 teaspoon Ac'cent flavor enhancer
½ teaspoon salt
¹⁄₁₆ teaspoon pepper
¾ cup chicken bouillon
¼ cup dry sherry
1 cup plain croutons
¼ cup grated Swiss cheese
¼ cup grated Parmesan cheese
1 tablespoon butter, melted

Heat corn oil in fry pan over medium heat. Add chicken and brown on all sides. Remove chicken to casserole. Add onions to fry pan in remaining oil and stir-fry about 2 minutes. Mix together flour, flavor enhancer, salt and pepper; add to onion. Add bouillon and sherry; stir. Pour over chicken, cover and bake in 350° oven about 1 hour or until fork can be inserted with ease. Uncover. Toss croutons with Swiss and Parmesan cheese and melted butter. Spread over chicken. Place under broiler just until cheese melts. Serve immediately. Makes 6 servings.

Ms. Carol R. Lacey, Reno, Nevada

New Hampshire

Your family will be very pleased when you serve this dish for dark meat lovers. The ring of cooked peas brightens its appearance and makes it a true meal-in-one.

CHICKEN DRUMSTICKS ON RICE PUERTO RICAN

8 broiler-fryer chicken drumsticks
2 teaspoons salt
1 teaspoon Ac'cent flavor enhancer
¼ teaspoon pepper
¼ cup Mazola corn oil
¾ cup chopped onion
2 cloves garlic, minced
1 green pepper, seeded, chopped
1 cup canned tomatoes, drained

1 bay leaf
2 cans (10¾ ounces each) chicken broth
¼ teaspoon curry powder
1 cup uncooked long grain rice
½ cup sliced green olives
1 package (10 ounces) frozen peas, cooked as package directs

Rub chicken with salt, flavor enhancer and pepper. Heat corn oil in fry pan over medium heat. Add chicken and brown on all sides. Transfer chicken to a large (3 quart) casserole. Add onion, garlic and green pepper to remaining corn oil in fry pan. Saute about 10 minutes. To this add tomatoes, bay leaf, chicken broth and curry. Bring to boil; pour over chicken. Add rice, cover and bake in 350° oven about 25 minutes or until fork can be inserted in chicken with ease and rice is tender. Remove bay leaf; sprinkle with olives. Place peas in circle around edge of dish. Makes 4 servings.

Mrs. Harold Parsons (Hilda), Bennington, New Hampshire

New Jersey

After a conventional baking period, these chicken parts are topped with some surprising ingredients and browned under the broiler. Nice and crusty!

CHICKEN DIABLO

2 broiler-fryer chickens, cut in parts
⅓ cup Mazola corn oil
2 teaspoons Ac'cent flavor enhancer
1 teaspoon salt
¼ teaspoon pepper
1 can (4½ ounces) deviled ham spread

1 tablespoon prepared mustard
2 teaspoons minced fresh parsley
4 drops hot pepper sauce
½ cup fine dry breadcrumbs
¼ teaspoon leaf thyme, crushed

Roll chicken in corn oil. Mix together flavor enhancer, salt and pepper. Sprinkle over chicken. Place chicken in single layer, skin side up, on rack in large shallow baking pan. (Drizzle any remaining corn oil over chicken.) Bake in 400° oven, uncovered, basting once or twice, about 40 minutes or until fork can be inserted with ease. Remove pan from oven; let cool about 5 minutes. Mix together ham spread, mustard, parsley and pepper sauce. Spread mixture evenly over chicken. Mix breadcrumbs and thyme; sprinkle lightly over chicken. Spoon pan drippings over breadcrumbs. Broil about 5 inches from heat, about 3 minutes, or until topping is nicely browned. Garnish with pepper rings and cherry tomatoes. Makes 8 servings.

Mrs. Frank A. Hornicek (Mildred), Dumont, New Jersey

New Mexico

Use your blender to prepare this internationally flavored marinade. An easy oven dish for four.

SESAME CHICKEN

1 broiler-fryer chicken, cut in parts
¼ cup Mazola corn oil
¼ cup soy sauce
3 tablespoons sesame seeds
2 tablespoons white cooking wine
1 clove garlic, peeled, halved
1 medium yellow onion, chopped
2 teaspoons brown sugar
1 teaspoon Ac'cent flavor enhancer
1 teaspoon red chili (medium hot)
¼ teaspoon powdered ginger

In blender container place corn oil, soy sauce, sesame seeds, wine, garlic, onion, brown sugar, flavor enhancer, chili and ginger. Cover and blend until liquefied, about 1 minute. Pour marinade into bowl; add chicken and marinate, mixing occasionally, at least 30 minutes. Place chicken in single layer, skin side up, in large shallow baking pan. Bake, uncovered, in 350° oven, basting occasionally, about 1 hour or until fork can be inserted with ease. Makes 4 servings.

Mrs. Hiroko Ortega, Santa Fe, New Mexico

New York

Here's a variation on the classic Chicken Kiev which uses chopped fresh mushrooms and shredded Cheddar. Though it takes advance preparation, it's a special dish which will please guests.

STUFFED CHICKEN BREASTS

3 whole broiler-fryer chicken breasts, halved, boned, skinned, pounded about ¼-inch thick
2 tablespoons butter
½ cup finely chopped fresh mushrooms
6 tablespoons flour, divided
½ cup light cream
1½ teaspoons Ac'cent flavor enhancer, divided

1¼ teaspoons salt, divided
1/16 teaspoon cayenne pepper
5 ounces sharp Cheddar cheese, shredded (about 1¼ cups)
2 eggs, slightly beaten
2/3 cup fine dry bread-crumbs
1 quart (about) Mazola corn oil

Melt butter in fry pan over medium heat. Add mushrooms and cook, stirring frequently, about 5 minutes. Stir in 2 tablespoons of the flour. Stir in cream, ½ teaspoon of the flavor enhancer, ¼ teaspoon of the salt and cayenne pepper, cooking about 2 more minutes. Stir in cheese; cook over very low heat, stirring constantly, until cheese melts. Turn mixture into pie plate. Cover; chill 1 hour. Cut mixture into 6 pieces; shape into short sticks. Sprinkle chicken with remaining flavor enhancer and salt. Place cheese stick on each piece. Tucking in sides, roll as for jelly roll. Press to seal well. Dust with remaining flour; dip in eggs, then roll in breadcrumbs. Cover and chill 1 hour. Heat corn oil in deep fryer (filling no more than ⅓ full) to 375°. Carefully place rolls, a few at a time, in hot corn oil. Fry about 5 minutes or until golden. Drain on paper towels. Place in a single layer in large shallow baking pan. Bake, uncovered, in 325° oven about 40 minutes or until fork can be inserted with ease. Makes 6 servings.

Ms. Darsene Baggett, New York, New York

North Carolina

Here's a "way out" flavor combination which is surprisingly good—chicken is teamed with the sweetness of pears and molasses and the punch of soy and ginger.

EVER'GOOD BARBECUED CHICKEN

1 broiler-fryer chicken, quartered
¾ cup pear nectar
⅓ cup soy sauce
¼ cup Mazola corn oil
¼ cup lemon juice
¼ cup molasses
1 teaspoon Ac'cent flavor enhancer
1 teaspoon ginger

In a bowl mix together pear nectar, soy sauce, corn oil, lemon juice, molasses, flavor enhancer and ginger. Brush chicken with sauce. Place chicken on grill, skin side up, about 8 inches from heat. Cook slowly, turning and brushing frequently about 1 hour or until fork can be inserted with ease. During last 15 minutes brush sauce on generously. Makes 4 servings.

Mrs. Dora M. Parnell, High Point, North Carolina

North Dakota

Browned chicken is steamed on a rice stuffing with the added texture of chopped pecans and the exciting flavor notes of orange and lemon juice, onion and pimento. A good start on an all-oven-meal.

BAKED CHICKEN WITH ORANGE NUT RICE

1 broiler-fryer chicken, cut in parts
1/3 cup flour
2 teaspoons salt, divided
1 teaspoon Ac'cent flavor enhancer
1/4 teaspoon white pepper
1/3 cup Mazola corn oil
1 cup water
1/2 cup orange juice
1/2 cup minced onion
1/4 cup butter, cut in pieces
2 tablespoons chopped pecans
2 tablespoons chopped pimento
1 tablespoon lemon juice
1 1/2 cups uncooked instant rice

Mix together flour, 1 teaspoon of the salt, flavor enhancer and white pepper. Coat chicken on all sides. Heat corn oil in fry pan over medium heat. Add chicken and brown on all sides. In large shallow baking pan put water, orange juice, onion, butter, pecans, pimento and lemon juice. Add rice and remaining salt. Stir to mix. Place chicken in single layer skin side up on rice. Cover with foil. Bake in 350° oven about 35 minutes. Uncover and bake about 15 minutes longer or until fork can be inserted with ease. Makes 4 servings.

Mrs. Oliver Halgunseth (Agnes), Abercrombie, North Dakota

Ohio

Mushroom lovers, attention! Here's a recipe designed just for you. Pickle relish adds interest and the dish also has a nice selection of herbs. Party perfect!

CHICKEN ROLL-UPS

4 whole broiler-fryer chicken breasts, halved, skinned, boned and flattened
¼ cup margarine, melted
1 small onion, finely chopped
1 stalk celery, finely chopped
1 can (4 ounces) sliced mushrooms, drained (liquid and 8 slices reserved), remainder finely chopped

1 cup breadcrumbs
⅓ cup sweet pickle relish
1 teaspoon Ac'cent flavor enhancer
½ teaspoon salt
¼ teaspoon dried marjoram
¼ teaspoon dried basil
¼ cup Mazola corn oil
1 can (10½ ounces) cream of mushroom soup

Saute onion, celery and chopped mushrooms in margarine about 5 minutes. Remove from heat. Add breadcrumbs, pickle relish, flavor enhancer, salt, marjoram and basil. Mix well. Place crumb mixture on chicken pieces, dividing evenly among the 8 pieces. Roll in jelly roll fashion. Tie each with string. In large shallow baking pan pour corn oil. Turn each roll to coat with corn oil. Bake, uncovered, in 400° oven about 50 minutes or until fork can be inserted with ease. Remove rolls from pan and remove strings. Blend mushroom soup and reserved mushroom liquid with pan drippings. Replace rolls in pan and spoon sauce over. Return to oven about 10 minutes or until sauce is hot. Serve chicken rolls with sauce and garnish with reserved mushroom slices. Makes 8 servings.

Mrs. Penny Sheely, Butler, Ohio

Oklahoma

Plan on using this chicken and macaroni salad as a main-dish star at a summer meal. Nice for a mixed buffet as well.

CRUNCHY CHICKEN SALAD

- 1 broiler-fryer chicken, simmered, skinned, boned and cut in bite-size pieces
- 3 cups cooked corkscrew macaroni
- 2 bunches green onions, chopped (use only small amount green portion)
- 1 cucumber, peeled, sliced (if unwaxed, may be unpeeled)
- 1 cup black olives, sliced
- ½ cup water chestnuts, sliced
- ¼ cup chopped pimento
- 1 teaspoon Ac'cent flavor enhancer
- 1 teaspoon salt
- ¼ teaspoon pepper
- ½ cup dairy sour cream
- ⅓ cup Mazola corn oil
- ¼ cup white vinegar

In large bowl place chicken, macaroni, onions, cucumber, olives, water chestnuts, pimento, flavor enhancer, salt and pepper; toss lightly. In small bowl mix together sour cream, corn oil and vinegar. Pour over chicken mixture and toss again lightly. Refrigerate 6 hours. To serve, place in lettuce lined salad bowl and top with sliced hard cooked egg. Makes 6 servings.

SIMMERED CHICKEN: Place 1 broiler-fryer chicken, whole or cut in parts, in kettle with 2 cups water. Add 1 small sliced onion, 3 celery tops, 1 teaspoon salt, 1 teaspoon Ac'cent flavor enhancer and ¼ teaspoon pepper. Bring to boil; cover tightly. Reduce heat and simmer 1 hour or until fork can be inserted with ease. Remove from heat; strain broth. Refrigerate chicken and broth. When chicken is cool, remove meat from bones and skin.

Miss Carolyn S. Williams, Tulsa, Oklahoma

Oregon

Here, frozen patty shell dough is used to make unique roll-ups with an artfully seasoned chicken filling. A nice surprise for company!

FRENCH CHICKEN PUFFS

2 broiler-fryer chicken breasts, halved, skinned
¼ cup flour
1 teaspoon Ac'cent flavor enhancer
½ teaspoon salt
¼ teaspoon pepper
7 tablespoons Mazola corn oil, divided
¼ pound mushrooms, sliced
¼ cup sliced ripe olives
1 can (10¾ ounces) cream of chicken soup
½ cup cream
2 tablespoons white wine
1 package (10 ounces) frozen patty shell, thawed

Mix together flour, flavor enhancer, salt, and pepper. Coat chicken. Heat ¼ cup of the corn oil in fry pan over medium heat. Add chicken and cook lightly, about 20 minutes, or until fork can be inserted with ease. When cool, remove meat from bone and cut in small pieces. Add 2 tablespoons of the remaining corn oil to fry pan; add mushrooms and cook until lightly brown. Add ripe olives. Mix mushroom-olive mixture with chicken. In a saucepan, place chicken soup, cream and wine, stirring constantly, until heated. Add to chicken mixture. On a floured board roll each patty shell to 7-8 inches diameter. Spread chicken mixture over pastry, dividing evenly among the 6 pastry pieces; turn side edges in to hold filling, roll individually, jelly roll fashion. Place on baking sheet, seam side down. Bake in 425° oven about 15 minutes. Brush tops with remaining corn oil and return to oven. Reduce heat to 325° and bake another 20 minutes. Cool about 5 minutes before serving. May be cut in pieces if desired. Makes 6 servings.

Mrs. Lynna Dean Kleinsmith, Portland, Oregon

Pennsylvania

The last touch—a topping of popular granola—creates a brand new taste for chicken breasts.

GRAN-OL-CHICKEN BAKE

3 whole broiler-fryer
  chicken breasts, halved,
  boned
1 teaspoon Ac'cent flavor
  enhancer
1 teaspoon salt
¼ teaspoon pepper

½ cup flour
⅓ cup Mazola corn oil
1 cup dairy sour cream
¼ cup raisins
1¼ cups granola cereal
2 tablespoons melted butter

Rub flavor enhancer into chicken. Sprinkle with salt and pepper; coat with flour. Heat corn oil in fry pan over medium heat. Add chicken and brown on all sides. Place chicken in single layer skin side up in large shallow baking pan. Spread with sour cream; sprinkle with raisins. Cover with foil and bake 30 minutes in 350° oven. Uncover; sprinkle with cereal. Sprinkle melted butter over cereal. Bake about 5 minutes until cereal is heated and fork can be inserted with ease. Makes 6 servings.

Miss Gloria T. Bove, Bethlehem, Pennsylvania

Rhode Island

If you dare to be different, you'll want to try this recipe. The red cabbage mixture adds a certain sweetness.

CHICKEN WITH RED CABBAGE, POLISH STYLE

1 whole broiler-fryer chicken
¼ cup Mazola corn oil
1½ teaspoons Ac'cent flavor enhancer
¼ teaspoon pepper
1 head (about 2½ pounds) red cabbage, coarsely shredded
1 small onion, chopped
½ teaspoon salt
¼ pound salt pork, cubed
½ cup red wine
Juice of 1 lemon
1 cup water

Mix together corn oil, flavor enhancer and pepper. Rub cavity and outside of chicken with mixture being sure to use it all. Place chicken, breast side up, in large shallow roasting pan. Roast in 425° oven, uncovered, 30 minutes or until nicely browned. Remove chicken and lower temperature to 350°. Mix together cabbage, onion and salt; let stand 10 minutes. Squeeze out liquid. In a fry pan cook salt pork until lightly browned. Add cabbage mixture, wine and lemon juice. Cover and simmer 20 minutes. Place cabbage loosely in cavity; cover with remaining cabbage. Pour water in bottom of pan. Cover pan tightly with foil and roast about 30 minutes or until fork can be inserted with ease. Makes 4 servings.

Mrs. Arthur T. Gately (Helen), Rumford, Rhode Island

South Carolina

Authoritative flavorings distinguish this broiled chicken recipe. Blue cheese lovers will enjoy it.

LEMON BLUE CHEESE CHICKEN

1 broiler-fryer chicken, quartered
½ cup Mazola corn oil
1 teaspoon grated lemon rind
¼ cup lemon juice
¼ cup crumbled blue cheese (approx. 2 ounces)
1 teaspoon Ac'cent flavor enhancer
1 teaspoon salt
½ teaspoon pepper

In bowl mix together corn oil, lemon rind, lemon juice, cheese, flavor enhancer, salt and pepper. Dip chicken in sauce. Place on broiler pan, skin side down, about 5-8 inches from heat. Cook, turning chicken frequently, basting with additional sauce, about 45 minutes or until browned and fork can be inserted with ease. Garnish with lemon slices. Makes 4 servings.

Miss Katherine Moss, Gaffney, South Carolina

South Dakota

The ingredients you add to this recipe for chicken parts resemble an excellent Italian dressing with a garlic accent. Only one pan to wash, too!

SAVORY CHICKEN SAUTE

1 broiler-fryer chicken, cut in parts
1 teaspoon Ac'cent flavor enhancer
¼ cup Mazola corn oil
4 cloves garlic, finely minced

1½ teaspoons salt
¼ teaspoon freshly ground black pepper
¼ cup red wine vinegar
1 teaspoon crumbled dried oregano leaves
¼ cup chopped parsley

Sprinkle chicken with flavor enhancer. Heat corn oil in fry pan over medium heat. Add garlic and cook 2 minutes. Add chicken and brown on all sides. Sprinkle with salt and pepper. Remove chicken; drain excess fat from pan. Return chicken to pan; add vinegar, oregano and parsley. Cover and cook very gently about 15 minutes; turn chicken and cook 15 minutes longer or until fork can be inserted with ease. Makes 4 servings.

Mr. Dan Darroch, Brandon, South Dakota

Tennessee

The combination of flavors in this recipe for chicken parts is completely unique—imagine honey and poultry seasoning in the same recipe!

TENNESSEE WALTZING CHICKEN

1 broiler-fryer chicken, cut in parts
½ cup flour
2 teaspoons Ac'cent flavor enhancer
1 teaspoon salt
1 teaspoon paprika
½ teaspoon poultry seasoning

¾ cup Mazola corn oil
½ cup catchup
¼ cup orange juice
1 tablespoon honey
1 teaspoon prepared mustard
1 teaspoon Worcestershire sauce

In a paper bag mix together flour, flavor enhancer, salt, paprika and poultry seasoning. Add chicken; shake to coat. Heat corn oil in fry pan over medium heat. Add chicken and brown on all sides. In a small saucepan stir together catchup, orange juice, honey, mustard and Worcestershire sauce. Simmer, stirring occasionally, about 5 minutes. Place chicken in single layer skin side up in large shallow baking pan. Spoon sauce over chicken. Bake in 350° oven, uncovered, about 20 minutes. Spoon on remaining sauce; bake about 20 minutes longer or until fork can be inserted with ease. Makes 4 servings.

Mrs. M. D. Starr (Tula), Memphis, Tennessee

Texas

The salty goodness of dried beef and cheddar cheese creates a baked-in flavor bonus for chicken thighs, always a good buy.

STUFFED CALICO CHICKEN THIGHS

12 broiler-fryer chicken thighs, boned, skinned and flattened
1 jar (2½) ounces dried beef, finely chopped
12 tablespoons shredded cheddar cheese
6 strips pimento, cut in half
12 strips bacon
2 eggs, slightly beaten

5 tablespoons lemon juice, divided
1 cup fine dry breadcrumbs
2 teaspoons lemon-pepper seasoning
1 teaspoon salt
1 teaspoon Ac'cent flavor enhancer
⅓ cup Mazola corn oil

Place 1 tablespoon dried beef, 1 tablespoon cheese and 1 piece pimento on each thigh. Fold sides and secure with wooden picks. Wrap bacon around open end and secure with picks. In one bowl mix eggs and 2 tablespoons of the lemon juice. In a second bowl mix together breadcrumbs, lemon-pepper seasoning, salt and flavor enhancer. Dip chicken in egg mixture then in breadcrumb mixture. Heat corn oil in fry pan over medium heat. Add chicken and brown on all sides. Place in single layer in large shallow baking pan; sprinkle with remaining lemon juice. Bake, uncovered, in 350° oven about 45 minutes or until fork can be inserted with ease. Makes 6 servings.

Mrs. Robert W. Sebastian (Beverly), Fort Worth, Texas

Utah

Sweet as a sunset on the beach at Waikiki—but piquant, too, with soy and ginger. Try this on your barbecue!

HONEYLULU CHICKEN B-B-Q

1 broiler-fryer chicken, cut in parts
½ cup sweetened pineapple juice
¼ cup soy sauce
¼ cup honey
¼ cup Mazola corn oil
1 teaspoon Ac'cent flavor enhancer
1 teaspoon seasoned salt
1 teaspoon ginger
1 teaspoon dry mustard
$\frac{1}{16}$ teaspoon freshly ground pepper

In a saucepan mix together pineapple juice, soy sauce, honey, corn oil, flavor enhancer, salt, ginger, mustard and pepper. Simmer 5 minutes. Cool. Brush each piece of chicken with marinade and place in single layer in large shallow baking pan; pour remaining marinade over chicken and marinate several hours or overnight. Place chicken on hot grill, skin side up, about 2 inches from heat. Cook, turning and basting often, 1 hour or until fork can be inserted with ease. Makes 4 servings.

Mrs. Gus Daskalakis (Mary), Salt Lake City, Utah

Vermont

These chicken thighs are baked on a mixture which will remind you of all the best of holiday feasting. All you need to complete the meal is a dish of crisp relishes.

CONFETTI CHICKEN

12 broiler-fryer chicken thighs
3 cups chicken broth
⅔ cup instant barley
1½ cups flour
1½ teaspoons baking powder
1½ teaspoons Ac'cent flavor enhancer, divided
1 egg, beaten
1 cup milk
1 quart (about) Mazola corn oil, divided

2 cups whole kernel corn
¾ cup diced raw celery
¾ cup diced raw carrot
½ cup chopped nuts
½ cup cranberry orange relish
1½ teaspoons poultry seasoning
1 teaspoon dried sweet basil

In a large oven-to-table casserole heat chicken broth to boiling. Stir in barley. Reduce heat, cover, and simmer 20 minutes. To make batter, stir together flour, baking powder, ½ teaspoon of the flavor enhancer, egg, milk and ⅓ cup of the corn oil. Coat chicken with batter. Pour corn oil in a deep fryer, filling utensil no more than ⅓ full. Heat corn oil over medium heat to 360°. Carefully add chicken, a few pieces at a time, to the hot corn oil and cook until brown. Drain well on paper towels. Remove barley from heat. Stir in corn, celery, carrot, nuts, relish, poultry seasoning, basil and remaining 1 teaspoon flavor enhancer. Arrange chicken in pinwheel fashion on vegetables in casserole. Bake, covered, in 350° oven 30 minutes. Uncover and increase temperature to 375° and bake 15 minutes or until fork can be inserted with ease. Makes 6 servings.

Mrs. Anita F. Gaiero, Vershire, Vermont

Virginia

The flavorings will remind you of chicken cacciatore, with capers adding an unusual touch.

MY FAVORITE THINGS CHICKEN

1 broiler-fryer chicken, cut in parts, skinned
1½ teaspoons Ac'cent flavor enhancer
⅔ cup flour
2 teaspoons paprika
1 teaspoon salt
⅓ cup Mazola corn oil

1 medium onion, sliced, rings separated
1 green bell pepper, cut in rings
1 can (11 ounces) whole tomatoes (Italian)
¼ cup capers, drained

Sprinkle chicken with flavor enhancer. In bag mix together flour, paprika and salt. Add chicken; shake to coat. Heat corn oil in fry pan over medium heat. Add chicken and brown lightly on all sides. Add onion, pepper, tomatoes and capers. Cover and cook on low heat about 40 minutes or until fork can be inserted with ease and sauce is thickened. Makes 4 servings.

Mrs. John N. Williams (Helen), Danville, Virginia

Washington

Many good chefs treasure secret barbecue sauces. Here's one being made public; lime juice and ginger give it a tropical tang.

BARBECUED CHICKEN

2 broiler-fryer chickens, cut in parts
2 tablespoons corn starch
2 cans (8 ounces each) tomato sauce
¾ cup Mazola corn oil
½ cup soy sauce
⅓ cup lime juice
2 tablespoons sugar
1 tablespoon garlic powder
2 teaspoons ground ginger
1 teaspoon Ac'cent flavor enhancer

In saucepan blend corn starch with part of the tomato sauce, gradually stirring in remaining tomato sauce, corn oil, soy sauce, lime juice, sugar, garlic powder, ginger and flavor enhancer. Cook, stirring constantly, until mixture boils. Boil about 2 minutes. Cool. Place chicken in large bowl and pour sauce over; cover and refrigerate 2 hours or longer. Place chicken in single layer, skin side up, on rack in large shallow baking pan. Bake in 350° oven, uncovered, basting several times, about 1 hour or until fork can be inserted with ease. Makes 8 servings.

Ms. Francine Stryker, Pacific Beach, Washington

West Virginia

Crackermeal makes a special crust for these chicken breasts. A cranberry-flavored barbecue sauce gives baked-in flavor and tenderness. A pretty dish to serve to a crowd.

SAUCY CRANBERRY CHICKEN

4 whole broiler-fryer chicken breasts, halved
2 teaspoons Ac'cent flavor enhancer, divided
½ cup flour
¼ cup crackermeal
¼ teaspoon salt
⅛ teaspoon pepper
⅛ teaspoon paprika
½ cup Mazola corn oil
1 can (16 ounces) jellied cranberry sauce
1 bottle (12 ounces) chili sauce
1 tablespoon brown sugar
1 tablespoon lemon juice

Sprinkle chicken with 1 teaspoon of the flavor enhancer. In a pie plate mix together flour, crackermeal, salt, pepper and paprika; coat chicken. Heat corn oil in fry pan over medium heat. Add chicken and brown on all sides. Place chicken in single layer, skin side up, in large shallow baking pan. In saucepan mix together cranberry sauce, chili sauce, brown sugar, lemon juice and remaining flavor enhancer. Cook over medium heat, stirring constantly, until cranberry sauce is melted and mixture is smooth. Spoon over chicken. Bake in 350° oven, uncovered, about 45 minutes or until fork can be inserted with ease. Makes 8 servings.

Mrs. Arietta L. Barnett, Charleston, West Virginia

Wisconsin

Here's an easy way to create a barbecue baste—with catchup and lemonade concentrate. Slow cooking insures perfection.

OUTDOOR LEMONY BARBECUED CHICKEN

2 broiler-fryer chickens, quartered
1¼ cups catchup
1 can (6 ounces) frozen lemonade, thawed, undiluted
¾ cup water
¼ cup Worcestershire sauce

¼ cup prepared yellow mustard
¼ cup Mazola corn oil
2 tablespoons instant minced onion
1 teaspoon Ac'cent flavor enhancer

In a saucepan stir together catchup, lemonade, water, Worcestershire sauce, mustard, corn oil, onion and flavor enhancer. Heat to boiling and simmer 5 minutes. Place chicken on grill, skin side up, about 8 inches from heat. Cook basting frequently and turning several times, about 1½ hours or until fork can be inserted with ease. Makes 8 servings.

Miss Maria Kuether, Milwaukee, Wisconsin

Wyoming

If you consider yourself a gourmet, yet appreciate cooking convenience-style, you should appreciate this recipe. Cream of chicken soup is the basis of the sauce—and just look at the interesting additions.

CHICKEN LUAU

1 broiler-fryer chicken, cut in parts
¼ cup Mazola corn oil
1 can (10½ ounces) cream of chicken soup
1 green pepper, seeded, cut in strips
½ cup pineapple tidbits
¼ cup sauterne wine
2 teaspoons curry powder
1 large clove garlic, minced
1 teaspoon Ac'cent flavor enhancer

Heat corn oil in fry pan over medium heat. Add chicken and brown on all sides. Place chicken in single layer, skin side up, in large shallow baking pan. In fry pan mix together soup, green pepper, pineapple, wine, curry powder, garlic and flavor enhancer. Heat and stir to blend. Pour sauce over chicken. Bake, uncovered, basting occasionally, in 350° oven about 1 hour or until fork can be inserted with ease. Serve over rice; top with slivered almonds. Makes 4 servings.

Ms. Mildred E. Cathcart, Cheyenne, Wyoming

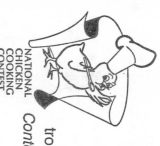

NATIONAL CHICKEN COOKING CONTEST

ENTRY BLANK

$10,000 - First Prize $ 3,000 - Third Prize
$ 4,000 - Second Prize $ 2,000 - Fourth Prize
            $ 1,000 - Fifth Prize

51 finalists win round trip to national cook-off plus $100 cash, trophy, year's supply of Ac'cent flavor enhancer and Mazola corn oil.

Contest Sponsored by: National Broiler Council along with the makers of Ac'cent® flavor enhancer and Mazola® corn oil.

SAMPLE RECIPE
CHICKEN BREASTS SUPREME

2 whole broiler-fryer chicken breasts, halved, boned, skinned
⅓ cup flour
1 teaspoon Ac'cent flavor enhancer
½ teaspoon salt
¼ teaspoon ground black pepper

¾ cup bread crumbs
3 tablespoons grated Parmesan cheese
½ cup finely chopped dried beef*
2 eggs, beaten
⅓ cup Mazola corn oil

Mix together flour, flavor enhancer, salt and pepper. Mix together bread crumbs, cheese and dried beef. Dip chicken in flour mixture; then egg; then crumb mixture. Heat corn oil in fry pan over medium heat. Add chicken. Cook over medium heat 10 minutes each side or until done. Makes 4 servings.
*May be done in blender or grinder.

Official Rules & Entry Form — National Chicken Cooking Contest

RULES

1. Predominant ingredient of recipe must be broiler-fryer (2-3½ lbs.) chicken (whole or any part or parts). Recipe must also include at least 1 teaspoon Ac'cent flavor enhancer and ¼ cup Mazola corn oil. Recipe must give amounts of principal ingredients and full instructions. If cooked chicken is ingredient, directions for cooking chicken must be given.

2. More than one entry per person permitted. Name, address, birth date and telephone number must be written on front page of each recipe. All entries must be postmarked by April 1 of contest year. None will be acknowledged or returned. OFFICIAL ENTRY FORM IS NOT REQUIRED.

3. Contestant must be at least 18 years of age and resident of United States. Employees and directors of National Broiler Council and their immediate families, and employees of Ac'cent and Mazola and their immediate families are not eligible.

4. One finalist from each state and D.C. will be selected through local cook-off or recipe judging-testing procedures. Finalist must be resident of state he or she is representing at time of national cook-off and must prepare recipe exactly as submitted for final evaluation at the national cook-off.

5. Judging will be on the basis of 5 equal points. They are: (1) simple enough to appeal to most people, (2) different enough to be interesting, (3) ingredients that are familiar and nationally available, (4) appearance, and (5) flavor.

6. Cost of transportation from contestant's home airport to the national cook-off and return will be paid. Room and meals at the national cook-off will be provided.

7. Recipes become the property of the National Chicken Cooking Contest with rights to adjust and edit. Decision of the judges is final. Taxes on prizes are responsibility of winner.

8. The National Chicken Cooking Contest is operated on a yearly basis, and the contest sponsors, jointly and individually, reserve the right to discontinue the contest or their sponsorship thereof, at the end of any contest year,

ENTRY FORM

Enter by sending us your recipe for broiler-fryer chicken.

Please mail to:
National Chicken Cooking Contest
614 Madison Building
1155-15th Street, N.W.
Washington, D.C. 20005

Recipe entry must be postmarked by April 1 of contest year.

Name: Mr. Mrs. Miss Ms. _____ _____ _____
(First-Given) (Middle) (Last)

Address _____ (Street or R.D.) _____

_____ _____ _____
(City) (State) (Zip Code)

Parent's or Spouse's Name _____ _____ _____
(First) (Middle) (Last)

Phone _____ (Please Include Area Code)

Birth Date _____

Recipe Title _____

INDEX

123

Kids love Chicken!
Grownups love Chicken!

Chicken is a fun food,
rich in protein, vitamins and
iron — low in cost. And, as this
cookbook shows, chicken is a
versatile meat to prepare.

Scientific advances in breeding,
nutrition and health have
helped farmers grow more
broilers with more meat on
their bones to satisfy
America's growing appetite
for chicken. And today's
broilers produce that meat
with less grain than any
other farm animal.

Eat some chicken today.
It's good for your family
and your budget.
American Cyanamid Company,
Agricultural Division —
nutrition and health
partner to the
poultry industry.